5⁹⁵
TAD

The English Civil War
A MILITARY HANDBOOK

The English
Civil War
A MILITARY HANDBOOK

Edited by John Tucker and Lewis S. Winstock

STACKPOLE BOOKS

Frontispiece:
A decorative framework from a seventeenth century military handbook Kriegskunst zu Fuss *by Johann Jacobi surrounding two illustrations from* The Commentaries of Sir Francis Vere *(1657).*
Top:
Tertios of an army advancing to give battle. This section from the Battle of Nieuport (1600) in The Commentaries of Sir Francis Vere *shows the manner of placing the musketeers at either end of the phalanx of pikes, still in use during the English Civil War.*
Below:
Tertios of musket and pike attacked by cavalry performing the caracole. This shows the way in which mutually-supporting tertios were used in seventeenth-century warfare.

Published by
Stackpole Books
Cameron and Kelker Streets
Harrisburg, Pa 17105

First published 1972
© The Sealed Knot Limited, 1972
© Lionel Leventhal Limited, 1972
All rights reserved

Printed in Great Britain

To N.R.F.T.

Library of Congress Cataloging in Publication Data

Tucker, John.
    The English Civil War.

    Bibliography: p.
    1. Great Britain--History--Civil War, 1642-1649.
I. Winstock, Lewis S., 1930-   joint author.
II. Title.
DA415.T797   942.06'2   72-2508
ISBN 0-8117-0545-5

contents

Foreword by Brigadier Peter Young   6
Editors' Introduction   7
Chronology 1642–1651 by David Chandler   8
Battles and Campaigns by David Gibbons   11
The Commanders by Norman Tucker   14
Colours and Heraldry by Brigadier Peter Young   23
Military Costume by Lieut-Col. J. B. R. Nicholson   29
Armour by Marcus Hinton   34
Weapons by Richard Ratner   40
Drill by Edward Surén   47
Artillery by Peter Morton   54
Siege Warfare by Christopher Duffy   65
The Role of the Navy by John Tucker   74
Bibliography by Lewis S. Winstock   79

FOREWORD
BY BRIGADIER PETER YOUNG

This book is intended as an introduction to the military history of the English Civil War. It is a piece of teamwork and the editors have tried to find an expert to deal with each of the various aspects of the war.

In the first place I should like to pay tribute to the late Norman Tucker who wrote the chapter 'The Commanders'. The historian on North Wales in the Civil War, this is the last of his many contributions to the history of these times and it is pleasant to be able to record that he took an enormous interest in this little book.

The Royal Military Academy at Sandhurst and its Department of War Studies is well represented by my former colleagues Dr. Christopher Duffy and David Chandler. Lieutenant-Colonel Nicholson who writes on costume is well known for his long and distinguished editorship of the magazine *Tradition*. Edward Suren and Marcus Hinton have both endeared themselves to the now numerous collectors of model soldiers by the lively series of figures which they have produced in recent years. This is a book as much for the wargamer and the lover of uniforms as for the historian in the true sense of the word. Richard Ratner who writes on weapons has one of the finest collections of ancient military firearms in private hands and, happily not stricken in years, he is on the way to being one of our foremost authorities. Peter Morton has an unrivalled knowledge of the artillery of the seventeenth century gained in the most practical way by building and employing, at countless battle re-enactments, the great guns 'Sweet Lips' and 'Magog'.

Editing has been in the capable hands of John Tucker, Lord Generall of the Parliamentarian forces of the Society who conceived the book, and Lewis S. Winstock, historian of the music of the British army.

The English Civil War was perhaps the most important single cataclysm in our history and it behoves us to study the period from every angle. If this book does something to point out unexplored paths and provide a perspective, then it will have achieved all that its authors hoped.

EDITORS' INTRODUCTION

There are many books on the English Civil War, and indeed the period can still kindle the flames of partisan feeling after more than three hundred years. Most serious works, however, deal with individual battles, campaigns, political history or are biographical, while a few definitive studies, such as Firth's *Cromwell's Army* delve deeply into the military structure of the time. But nowhere does there exist a concise and balanced introduction to the military aspects of the war. That is what this book attempts to provide.

In the pages available it would have been impossible to have covered the whole subject area, even in brief, and there are inevitably gaps: nevertheless, it is hoped that this book will serve as a worthwhile introduction to students of the period. Care has gone into the select bibliography, which points the way to further reading. While many of the illustrations are contemporary, every effort has been made to introduce new or little used material.

The book is unusual in that every contributor is a member of the Sealed Knot, a society which, as an Educational Charity, reenacts battles of the period—frequently on their original sites. This is reflected in a freshness of approach which helps to make the shadowy figures of our forebears more substantial.

The very special contribution of David Gibbons, the publisher's Chief Editor—himself a devotee of the period—has been most gratefully welcomed.

Valuable help has also come from Stephen Beck, an artist with a great feeling for the Civil War who has drawn some delightful sketches for the book; Dan Escott, who has produced three beautiful heraldic drawings; Philip Stearns for many photographic excursions; and John Walter, who has contributed several excellent drawings of lock-plates. The bulk of the contemporary illustrations come from books at the Royal Artillery Institution Library, Woolwich, and the Guildhall Library, London; the staffs of both libraries deserve a special mention of thanks for their patience and help.

Finally, the Editors would like to acknowledge particularly the guidance of Brigadier Peter Young, who kindly read the completed manuscript and made invaluable comments from his unrivalled knowledge of the period.

CHRONOLOGY 1642|1651

by David Chandler

From the day King Charles I raised his standard at Nottingham (22 August, 1642) to that on which his successor, King Charles II, departed from Shoreham Creek (15 October, 1651), the British Isles were in the grip of that most terrible of national experiences—civil war. The nine years were not filled with continuous strife; there were several pauses, and at different times different regions knew peace of a sort, but always there was tension, rumour and uncertainty.

The First (or 'Great') English Civil War lasted from 1642 until 1646, when, on 21 March, Sir Jacob Astley surrendered the last Royalist army at Stow-in-the-Wold. Then, after a year of bickering, intrigue and fruitless negotiation, occurred the Second Civil War (1647–8), which was brought to a close effectively by the battle of Preston and the surrender of Colchester in August, although a few Royalist garrisons continued to hold out for some further time before capitulating. The trial and execution of Charles I ensued, and this in turn was followed by what is sometimes termed the Third Civil War, comprising Cromwell's expedition to Ireland (1649–50), his campaign in Scotland (1650) and the final round in this long-drawn-out tale of internecine struggle, the Worcester campaign of 1651.

1642
3 January	King Charles attempts to arrest the Five Members
23 April	The King is refused admittance to Hull
4 July	Establishment of the Committee of Safety
21 August	Dover Castle surprised by the Roundheads
22 August	Nottingham. The King sets up his Standard
7 September	Goring surrenders Portsmouth to *Sir William Waller*
23 September	Powick Bridge. Prince Rupert routs the Parliamentarians
23 October	Edgehill. The King defeats the *Earl of Essex*
29 October	The Royalists occupy Oxford, which becomes their 'capital'
12 November	Prince Rupert storms Brentford
13 November	Turnham Green. *Essex* and the Trained Bands outface the Royalist army, which retires
6 December	Tadcaster. *Lord Fairfax* repulses Newcastle
12 December	*Waller* captures Winchester

1643
19 January	Braddock Down. Sir Ralph Hopton clears Cornwall
2 February	Prince Rupert storms Cirencester
23 February	The Queen lands at Bridlington
19 March	Hopton Heath. Northampton defeats *Gell* and *Brereton* but is slain
30 March	Seacroft Moor. Goring defeats *Sir Thomas Fairfax*

13 April	Ripple Field. Prince Maurice defeats *Waller*
21 April	Rupert takes Lichfield
23 April	Launceston. Hopton defeats *Chudleigh*
25 April	Caversham Bridge. Royalists fail to relieve Reading which falls on 27 April
25 April	Sourton Down. *Chudleigh* defeats Hopton
13 May	Grantham. *Cromwell* defeats Cavendish
16 May	Stratton. Hopton defeats *Stamford*
21 May	Storming of Wakefield. *Sir Thomas Fairfax* surprises Goring
18 June	Chalgrove Field. Rupert defeats *Stapleton* and *Hampden*. The latter is slain
29 June	Adwalton Moor. Newcastle destroys the army of the *Fairfaxes*
5 July	Lansdown. Hopton defeats *Waller*
13 July	Roundway Down. Wilmot, Hopton and Prince Maurice destroy *Waller's* army
26 July	Storming of Bristol. Colonel Nathaniel Fiennes surrenders to Rupert
27 July	Gainsborough. *Cromwell* defeats Cavendish who is slain
10 August to 4 September	King Charles besieges *Massey* in Gloucester which is relieved by *Essex*
6 September	Maurice takes Exeter
18 September	Aldbourne Chase. Prince Rupert harries *Essex*
20 September	First Newbury. King Charles is foiled by *Essex*, who continues his march to London
25 September	Solemn League and Covenant signed
6 October	Maurice takes Dartmouth
11 October	Hull. Newcastle raises his siege
11 October	Winceby. *Manchester*, *Sir Thomas Fairfax* and *Cromwell* defeat Sir William Widrington and Sir John Henderson
9 December	Hopton takes Arundel Castle

1644

6 January	*Waller* recaptures Arundel Castle
19 January	The Scots cross the border in support of Parliament
25 January	Nantwich. *Sir Thomas Fairfax* defeats Lord Byron and raises the siege
5 February	Corbridge. Langdale beats the Scots away
21 March	Relief of Newark. Rupert captures *Sir John Meldrum* and his army
29 March	Cheriton (Alresford). *Waller* defeats Lord Forth and Hopton
11 April	Colonel John Belasyse defeated and captured by *Fairfax* at Selby
6 May	*Manchester* storms Lincoln
25 May	Rupert storms Stockport
27 May	Rupert storms Bolton
11 June	Rupert takes Liverpool
29 June	Cropredy Bridge. The King defeats *Waller*
2 July	Marston Moor. The armies of the *Earl of Leven* (Scots), *Manchester* and *Fairfax* defeat Rupert and Newcastle. The North is virtually lost to the King
July	Alastair MacDonald and 1600 of his clan from Ireland arrive in Scotland and join the Marquis of Montrose
16 July	Sir Thomas Glemham surrenders York to the Scots and Parliamentarians
21 August	Beacon Hill near Lostwithiel. King Charles defeats *Essex*
31 August	Castle Dore near Fowey. King Charles defeats *Essex* who escapes by sea leaving his army under *Skippon* to surrender (2 Sept)
1 September	Tippermuir. Montrose routs *Lord Elgin's* Covenanters
13 September	Aberdeen. Montrose defeats *Lord Burleigh's* Covenanters
20 October	The Scots take the City of Newcastle
27 October	Second Newbury. The King, outnumbered, holds off *Manchester* and *Waller*
6 November	Rupert is made Lieutenant General of all the King's armies
9 November	Rupert relieves Donnington Castle
19 December	Self-Denying Ordinance/April 3 1645 Lords pass

1645

10 January	Rupert foiled in attempt to retake Abingdon
2 February	Montrose cuts up *Clan Campbell* at Inverlochy under the eyes of its Chief the *Marquis of Argyll*
19 February	Maurice relieves Chester
22 February	*Colonel Thomas Mytton* takes Shrewsbury
Early April	The New Model Army is formed from those of *Manchester*, *Essex* and *Waller* who resign their commands
4 April	Montrose takes Dundee
22 April	Rupert surprises *Massey* at Ledbury
24 April	*Cromwell* routs Northampton at Islip and captures Bletchington House
29 April	*Cromwell* attempts to take Faringdon Castle by escalade and is repulsed
9 May	Auldearn. Montrose defeats *Hurry's* Covenanters
30 May	Royalists storm Leicester
14 June	Battle of Naseby. The New Model Army under *Sir Thomas Fairfax* and *Cromwell* defeats the King and destroys his infantry and artillery
17 June	*Fairfax* takes Leicester
2 July	Alford. Montrose defeats *Baillie's* Covenanters
10 July	Battle of Langport. *Sir Thomas Fairfax* defeats Goring
23 July	*Sir Thomas Fairfax* captures Bridgewater
1 August	Colby Moor. *Laugharne* defeats Stradling's Pembrokeshire Royalists
10 September	Rupert surrenders Bristol to *Fairfax*
13 September	Philiphaugh: Montrose beaten
24 September	Rowton Heath. Royalists defeated before Chester
15 October	Basing House falls to *Cromwell*

1646

13 March	Hopton surrenders to *Fairfax* at Falmouth
21 March	Stow-in-the-Wold. Lord Astley surrenders last Royalist army
5 May	King surrenders to the Scots at Southwell
5 June	Benburb. O'Neill's Irish Royalists defeat *Monro's* Covenanters
25 June	Oxford surrenders

1647

8 August	Dunganhill (Ireland). *Colonel Michael Jones* routs the Irish

1648

17–19 August	Preston. *Cromwell* defeats the Duke of Hamilton's Royalists and Scots
28 August	Colchester. Royalist garrison (besieged since 12 June) surrenders to *Fairfax*

1649

30 January	Beheading of Charles I
2 August	Rathmines. Duke of Ormonde's Royalists fail to storm Dublin
12 September	Drogheda. Besieged since 3rd, falls to *Cromwell*. Garrison massacred
November	Waterford besieged by Cromwell
December	Broken off, then capitulates to Ireton 10 August 1650
23 September–16 October	Wexford besieged by *Cromwell*, then stormed

1650

27 April	Carbisdale. *Colonel Strachan* routs Montrose's Scottish Royalists
31 August	Haddington. Leslie routs *Cromwell's* rearguard but is repulsed
3 September	Dunbar. *Cromwell* defeats Leslie and the Covenanters
24 December	Edinburgh Castle (besieged since 4 September) falls to the New Model Army

1651

26 August	Wigan. *Lilburne* defeats Lord Derby's forces
28 August	Upton-on-Severn. *Lambert* defeats Massey's Royalists
3 September	Worcester. *Cromwell* defeats King Charles II and the Anglo-Scottish army
15 October	Charles II leaves Shoreham Creek for exile

Battles and Campaigns

by David Gibbons

the 'first' civil war

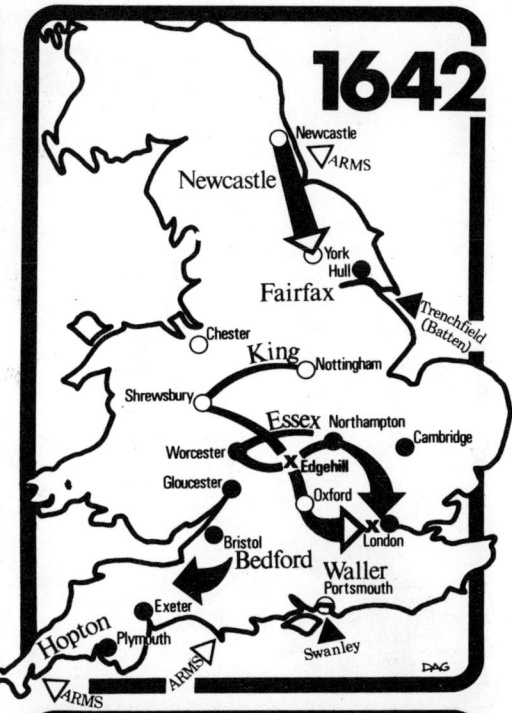

KEY TO THE MAPS

General Routes of the Main Armies:

◄ Royalist   ◄ Parliament

Towns, Cities, Castles held by:

○ Royalists   ● Parliament

Naval Operations, Seaborne Supplies:

◁ Royalist   ◀ Parliament

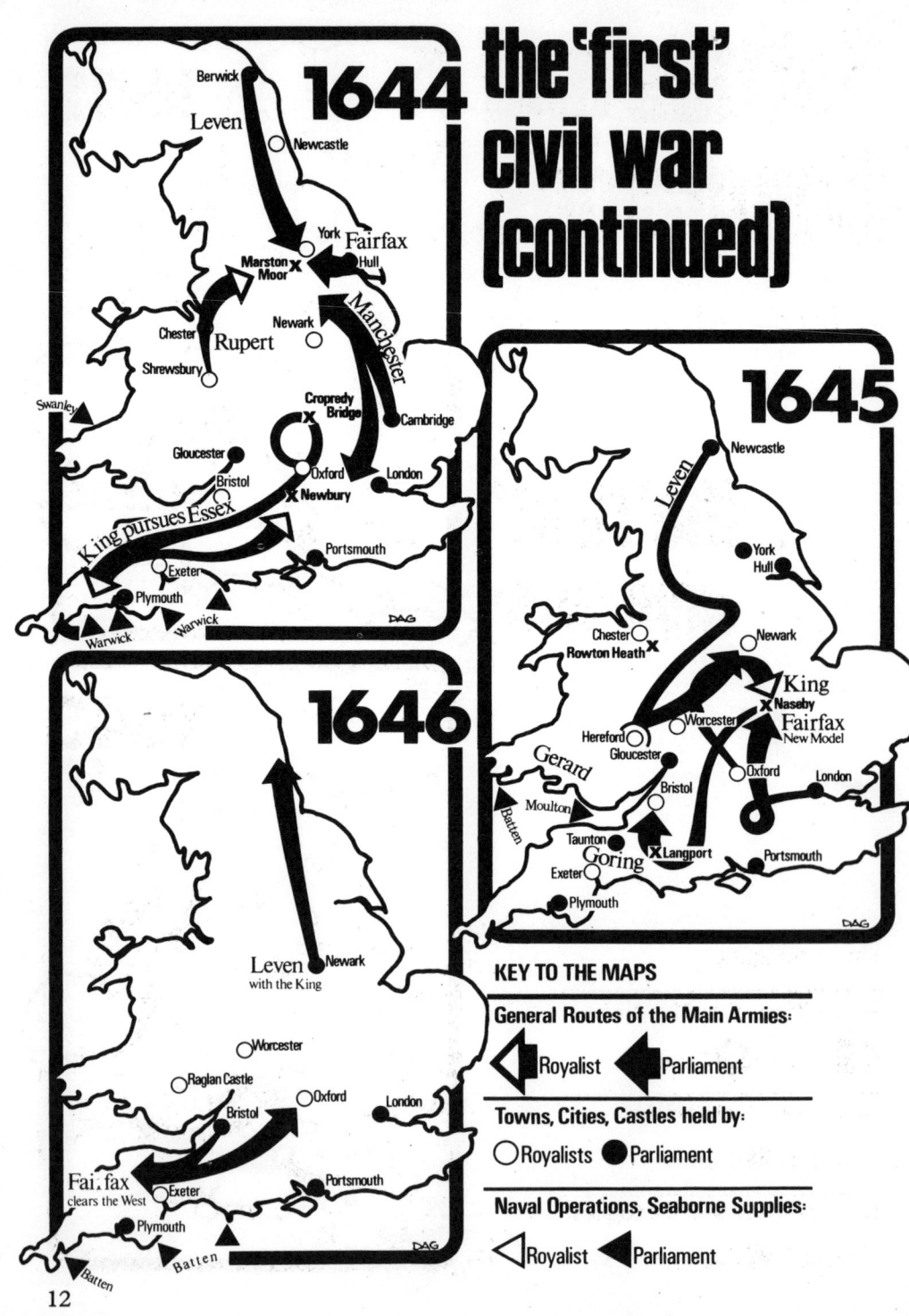

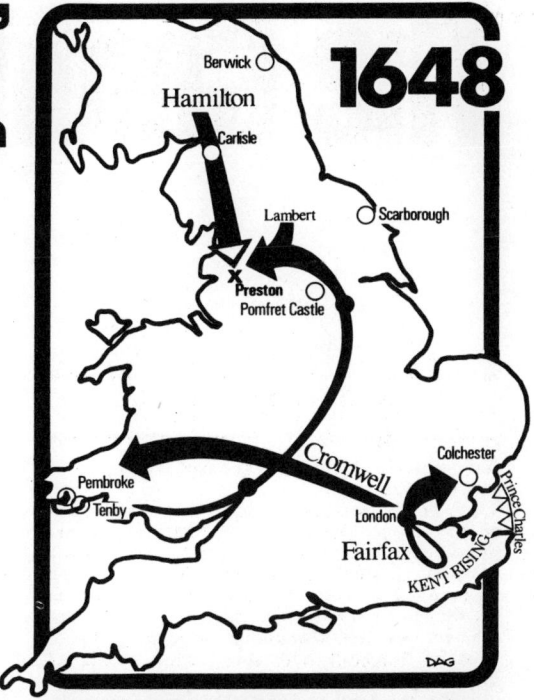

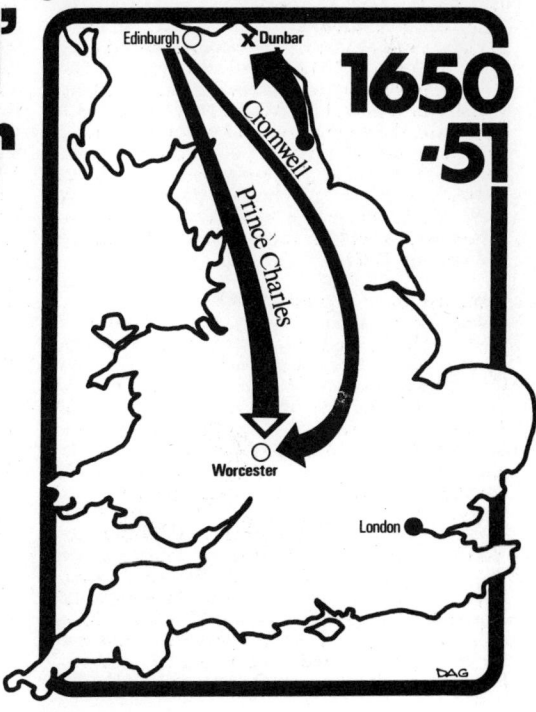

The Commanders

by Norman Tucker

ROYALIST

Sergeant-Major-General Lord Astley (1579–1652)
Came of a Norfolk family and served as a soldier of fortune in Denmark, the Netherlands and Germany. Returned to England and made governor of Plymouth in 1638. When the first Bishops' War was inevitable he was sent to Newcastle to oppose the Scots. Served under Charles I in Civil War and gained a knighthood. Was at Edgehill and the second battle of Newbury. Helped to besiege Gloucester and to capture Reading and Arundel. Was with the King when he escaped from Oxford. He commanded the Royalist foot at Naseby having been made a baron in 1644. He surrendered the last Royal army in the field to Sir William Brereton at Stow-in-the-Wold in March 1646. Rushworth states that the veteran seated himself on a drum and addressed his captors: 'You have now done your work and may go play unless you fall out among yourselves'. An 'honest, plain and brave man', Clarendon terms him. After a short imprisonment he was released and died at Maidstone in February 1652.

John, 1st Lord Byron (d. 1652)
Eldest son of Sir John Byron, K.B., of Newstead Abbey, Notts., and the senior of six brothers, all Royalist officers. Campaigned in the Low Countries and against the Scots. Created K.B. at the Coronation. In 1639 succeeded Colonel Lunsford as Governor of the Tower for some months. Rode to Oxford where he collected the plate, and horsed as many students as possible for the King's service. At Worcester he joined Rupert's force and at Powick Bridge participated in the first defeat of a Parliamentary force. Commanded the cavalry reserve at Edgehill and followed Rupert in the pursuit. Played a prominent part in the first battle of Newbury, 20 September 1643. On 24 October the King created him Baron Rochdale and Field Marshal for North Wales and several border counties. He joined his uncle, Sir Nicholas Byron, governor of Chester, and when several regiments under Royalist officers arrived from Ireland he mustered them to attack the Parliamentary headquarters in Cheshire. Successful at first, Nantwich proved too strong for him to take, and the Byronians were defeated by the joint forces of Sir Thomas Fairfax and the local commander, Sir William Brereton. When Sir Nicholas Byron was captured at Ellesmere in January following, Lord Byron became governor of Chester. He left temporarily to follow Rupert on his famous march through Lancashire which ended at Marston Moor where Byron had command of the right wing which was defeated by Cromwell. In September, Byron was again defeated before Montgomery Castle. On 23 September 1645, King Charles arrived in Chester which Byron had held stubbornly against Brereton's assaults. The following day Charles witnessed the defeat of his force who fled from Rowton Heath nearby. On departing for Denbigh the King told Byron that if he was not relieved in ten days he might make the best terms he could. It was not until 3 February, 1646, that Byron surrendered. He led his force to Caernarvon which he defended until 6 June, 1646. His second wife, sister of the gallant Royalist Sir Charles Lucas, shared his privations. In the spring of 1648 Byron was commissioned Commander-in-Chief of the area and sent to raise forces by the exiled Prince of Wales. Byron failed to take Shrewsbury or any of the Welsh castles. When Anglesey Royalists refused to serve under him he returned to France where he died childless in August 1652, the peerage passing to his brother Sir Richard.

Arthur, Baron Capel (1610–1649)
Of Hadham, Herts. Created a peer in 1641 and served in Parliament. In 1642 appointed Lieutenant-General under the 12-year-old Prince of Wales in command of North Wales and four Border shires. Headquarters at Shrewsbury where he appears to have had a press for propaganda. Active in Chesire and Shropshire without much success. Defeated by Mytton when he attacked Wem, October 1643. Lord Byron planned to supplant him. Sent to West

Country to join Lord Hopton, his uncle. Was one of the Committee appointed to assist the young Prince of Wales with headquarters at Bristol. Escorted the Queen to Paris and later helped King Charles to escape from Hampton Court. Joined in the revolt in the south-east during second Civil War. Defended Colchester when attacked by Fairfax, was captured and executed 9 March 1649. On the scaffold he gave his sword to Sir John Owen. It is still preserved in Lord Harlech's family.

Robert Dormer, Earl of Carnarvon (c. 1607–1643)

Lieutenant-General of Horse. Served in the West. Helped to capture Bristol. Overran Dorset, capturing Dorchester (4 August), Weymouth, and Portland. Was killed at the first battle of Newbury, 20 September 1643.

Sir Thomas Glemham (d. 1649)

Defended York gallantly in 1644 but was forced to negotiate a surrender. Rupert made him principal commander in the north. Rallied 3,000 for action in his area. Defended Carlisle gallantly but unsuccessfully. Rejoined the King in South Wales only to be offended when the King conferred a barony on Gerard which would have been better bestowed on Glemham. An expert in defending doomed cities Glemham was made governor of Oxford when all hope had gone; he watched the disguised King flee from the East Gate, 27 April 1646.

George, Lord Goring (1608–1657)

Son of the Earl of Norwich. Served in the Dutch forces in the Thirty Years War and at the siege of Breda (1637) received a wound in the ankle which left a permanent limp. When Civil War threatened he returned to England and Parliament made him governor of Portsmouth. He kept in touch with Queen Henrietta Maria, surrendered his charge, and threw in his lot with the King. He was best as a cavalry leader. At Seacroft Moor on 30 March 1643 Goring by a spirited charge inflicted on Sir Thomas Fairfax 'one of his greatest losses'. Goring's greatest achievement was his charge at Marston Moor 1644 when, as General of the left wing, he swept the Parliamentarians from the field, almost turning the fortunes of the day. Goring was captured at Wakefield, 21 May 1643. Having obtained his freedom, Goring the following year replaced Wilmot as General of Horse in charge of operations in the West Country. In July, 1645 Goring threatened Taunton which caused Fairfax to despatch additional men for reinforcements. Goring, trying to hold the pass at Langport, was defeated by a superior force but he escaped with a greater part of his army. This defeat broke the Royalist morale in the West. Goring as a fighting general made a name for himself, but he also gained a reputation for gaming, drinking and harshness. The plundering by his troopers made his name hated. For endeavouring to raise Kent in the Second Civil War he was condemned to lose his head with the Duke of Hamilton, Earl Holland, Lord Capel, and Sir John Owen, but the lives of Owen and Goring were spared. Goring secured his freedom and died in Madrid.

Sir Ralph (later Baron) Hopton, (1598–1652)

Born at Witham Friary, Somerset, admitted to the Middle Temple 1614, and later to Oxford. Served in the Palatinate during earlier part of the Thirty Years War, as a fellow officer of Waller, his future opponent. Elected M.P. for Shaftesbury 1621. Served in the regiment of Sir Charles Rich under Mansfeld in 1624. M.P. for Bath 1625. Was made K.B. at Coronation of Charles I. In 1639 acted as captain of the Royal bodyguard. In August 1642 was declared 'delinquent' by Parliament and later termed 'traitor'. The King appointed him Lieutenant-General of the West and Hopton proved himself next to Rupert the ablest of the royal commanders. In January 1643 he defeated Ruthin at Braddock Down and followed by taking Saltash and saved Cornwall for the King. His victory against odds at Stratton Hill in May was a triumph. He defeated Waller at Lansdown (5 July 1643), but was nearly killed by the accidental explosion of an ammunition cart, a double disaster as it robbed the force of its powder as well as its commander who, however, tried to direct operations from a sick bed. Hastening to his aid Lord Wilmot, Maurice, and Byron, defeated Waller at Roundway Down on 13 July. Hopton recovered to assist in the capture of Bristol 26 July, and on 4 September was created Baron Hopton of Stratton. In 1644 Waller defeated him at Cheriton. Hopton joined the King. In 1645 he was made General of the Ordnance, and the following year took command of the army under the Prince of Wales. He was defeated by Fairfax at Torrington and surrendered to Fairfax 14 March. He died at Bruges in 1652. After the Restoration his body was interred at his home.

Sir Marmaduke (later Baron) Langdale (1598–1661)

'A grave and very thin Yorkshireman, with long solemn face, brave as a lion, and both judicious and enterprising, but with an unfortunate temper.' This description by Markham is confirmed by Langdale's portrait. A professional soldier, knighted by King Charles in 1627. Though he had opposed ship-money he did not hesitate to join the King when war was imminent and became one of the most dependable cavalry leaders. Defeated the Scots cavalry at Corbridge in 1644 and fought at Marston Moor. Early in March 1645 he relieved Pontefract but his rapacious troopers antagonised the district. His most brilliant exploit was his defeat of Rossiter at Melton Mowbray in February 1645. At Naseby he commanded the Royalist left wing but saw his men scattered by Cromwell's charge. When, in September, Charles marched for Chester he was escorted by Sir Marmaduke and two other brigades of horse. At Holt the army divided, the

15

King's portion going down the left bank of the Dee to enter the city by the old bridge. Langdale, unaware that a Parliamentary force under Sydenham Poyntz was on his heels, crossed the bridge at Holt. The following day (24 September) after beating back his pursuers at Hatton Heath, he was trapped after a sally from the city and defeated on Rowton Heath. He rallied his men and operated in Wales where he appears for a while to have acted as Royalist commander. He moved north and when his forces were beaten at Carlisle he escaped to the Isle of Man. In the Second Civil War he crossed to Scotland to unite with the Duke of Hamilton. He fought well at Preston (17 August 1648) endeavouring, with 3,000 foot and 600 horse, to withstand Cromwell's unexpected attack, but was defeated after four hours fight. 'One of the finest feats of arms in the war', comments John Buchan. On 25 August he was captured near Nottingham. He escaped to the Continent and served with the Venetians against the Turks. When in Bruges in 1658 he was created Baron Langdale by Charles II. He died at Holme, 5 August, 1661. His estates had been confiscated but the title descended to his son, Marmaduke.

Colonel Will Legge (1609–70)

Professional soldier with undoubted fighting qualities is best remembered for his fidelity to Rupert. At Edgehill he rode into a troop similar to his own and was taken prisoner. Wounded in attack on Lichfield, but was well enough to lead the forlorn hope at Chalgrove Field. Helped to capture Bristol in July. In 1644 when Rupert marched to Marston Moor served as temporary governor of Chester in absence of Lord Byron. Made governor of Oxford 1645, but removed for no other reason than that of being Rupert's friend. Tried to reconcile Rupert and the King.

Robert Bertie, Earl of Lindsey, K.G., K.B. (1572–1642)

Lieutenant-General at Edgehill. Was mortally wounded in the battle. His son, Lord Willoughby d'Eresby of the King's Lifeguard, was captured while trying to rescue his dying father.

Sir George Lisle (d. 1648)

Fought at Cheriton, 29 March 1644, as Colonel of Horse. In charge of a brigade at the second battle of Newbury (27 October 1644). Fought gallantly, flinging off his buffcoat so that his white shirt indicated his leadership in the gloaming. In the Second Civil War was one of the defenders of Colchester. After its surrender was shot (in company with Sir Charles Lucas), for breaking parole, facing death with heroic fortitude.

Sir Charles Lucas (1613–48)

Began as Lieutenant-Colonel and rose to be Lieutenant-General. Participated in Rupert's charge at Powick Bridge where he was wounded. Fought at Edgehill. Commanded a brigade of horse against the Scots at encounter near Sunderland. Went to assist Rupert in the relief of York. Supported Goring in his successful charge at Marston Moor. In the Second Civil War he defended Colchester and after its capture he was shot for breaking parole, dying as bravely as he had fought.

Charles Gerard, Viscount Macclesfield (d. 1694)

Son of Sir Charles Gerard of Halsall, Lancashire. Trained in foreign parts and was a captain in Colonel Goring's regiment in 1640. When Charles mustered his army at Shrewsbury in September 1642 he was joined by Captain Charles Gerard with a foot regiment he had raised at his own expense. At Edgehill he commanded a brigade of foot which he fought with consummate skill. A friend and follower of Rupert whom he resembled in temperament. Helped to take Lichfield where he was wounded, and was active in the capture of Bristol, 26 July 1643. Was at the first battle of Newbury. The following year he aided Rupert to capture Newark (12 March 1644), where he was again wounded. By this time he was Major-General. His horse being brought down he was captured and was the means of arranging a surrender of the town. Later in 1644 Gerard was sent by Rupert to succeed the Earl of Carbery as commander in South Wales where the King's affairs were not progressing. He landed 'his Irish and Popish forces' at Black Rock, Monmouthshire, and marched to Haverfordwest, capturing castles and towns on his route. Despite his activity he found time to assist Rupert to relieve Beeston Castle in Cheshire. He returned to South Wales where his arrogance and the cruelty of his troops alienated the people. Protests to the King by leading Royalists resulted in Gerard and his officers being removed, and Sir Jacob Astley put in place of Gerard who was mollified by a peerage. At the head of a brigade of horse Lord Gerard escorted the King from Cardiff as far as Chester at the time of Rowton Heath, where he was again wounded. When Rupert was reproached by King Charles for surrendering Bristol, Gerard sided with the Prince and followed him into exile. 'This standing by his friend and benefactor' writes J. Roland Phillips, 'is the only noble trait I have been able to discover in Gerard's character'. He was subsequently rewarded by being created Earl of Macclesfield.

Prince Maurice (1621–1652)

Son of the Elector Palatine (King of Bohemia) and Elizabeth, sister of Charles I. Named after the Prince of Orange who gave shelter to the fugitive Queen of Bohemia. Served in Thirty Years War in the trenches before Breda with his brother Rupert, with whom he took ship to Newcastle to join Charles at Nottingham when war was declared. Wounded in the charge at Powick Bridge at the beginning of the war, and again at Edgehill. In the spring of 1643 Maurice advanced to the west, gaining a victory over Waller at Ripple Field near Tewkesbury (13

April). Was at Lansdown and Roundway Down and helped Rupert to take Bristol. When Chester was in danger Maurice was sent to raise the siege which he did on 19 February, remaining at Chester until 18 March. Created Sir John Owen a Major-General during his stay at Ruthin where the town minutes still record beer served to Maurice's troopers. Maurice returned to the West. His failure to capture Lyme (tenaciously defended by Colonel Robert Blake for two months) counted against Maurice. He took Exeter on 4 September, and Dartmouth on 6 October but was checked at Plymouth. Prominent in the Lostwithiel campaign. Fought in the second battle of Newbury 27 October, and helped to extricate the King's army. Maurice was in the first line during Rupert's charge at Naseby. After Rupert had surrendered Bristol to Fairfax, Maurice was present at the unhappy scene with Charles when the King refused to hear Rupert's explanation and he followed his elder brother into exile. During the Second Civil War, Maurice took to the sea as naturally as Rupert had done. He served off the Irish Coast, in the Mediterranean and in the West Indies until he went down when his ship, the *Honest Seaman*, sank in a storm with all hands. Clarendon's comment was that Maurice understood 'little of war than to fight very stoutly', Clennell Wilkinson, classifies him as brave and stubborn, a 'sort of Rupert without steel'.

General George Monk (later Duke of Albemarle) (1606–1670)

Born Potheridge, Devon, son of Sir Thomas Monk. Professional soldier. Early in life he served against Spain and France but in 1639 went to the Netherlands where he acquired experience and fame in the Thirty Years War. Interested in politics, he returned to help Charles I against the Scots. In 1641 he crossed to Ireland and was actively employed there until the close of 1643. Served under Byron in the attack on Nantwich in January 1644 where he was captured by Fairfax and Brereton. Accused by the House of high treason he was sent to the Tower where he remained for two years. While there he wrote *Observations upon Military and Political Affairs*. When the First Civil War ended he felt, as a soldier of fortune, free to join the Parliamentary army. He returned to Ireland and served as governor of Ulster until 1649 when he displeased Parliament by concluding in May that year a three months armistice with Owen Roe O'Neill, the Irish guerilla leader which reduced the pressure on his troops and prevented the Royalist Lord Lieutenant, Ormonde, from gaining control. But Monk had to surrender and on his return Parliament 'utterly disapproved' of the arrangement. He lost the regiment and went home in chagrin. Monk, however, seems to have convinced Cromwell that he had acted for the best for when Oliver returned from his Irish campaign, he gave Monk a new regiment, and made him Lieutenant-General of Ordnance. Monk contributed to the victory at Dunbar. When Cromwell left Scotland in 1641 he left Monk in charge of 8,000 troops in Scotland where the Highlands were still unsettled. Monk was made one of the Generals-at-Sea and proved himself a doughty fighter against the Dutch. The sea service ended, he returned to fight against the Royalists in Scotland and was there when Cromwell died in 1658. After the downfall of Richard Cromwell as Protector, Monk was responsible for bringing about the Restoration. Crossing the Coldstream River at the Border he led his regiment to London, earning for the 2nd Guards the name they have borne ever since. Charles II made him Duke of Albemarle and heaped honours on him. In 1664-6 he was again at sea and fought in the Battle of the Downs. He died on 3 January 1670 and was buried in Westminister Abbey.

James Graham, Marquis of Montrose, (1612–1650)

In 1637 took an active part in drawing up the National Covenant but soon broke away from the Presbyterians. Though he fought against the King in the first Bishops' War, 1640, after pardon he turned Royalist. When the Scots in 1644 entered into an alliance with the Parliament, Montrose in the Highlands raised a small force of some 2,000 men, and gained victory after victory but was finally routed at Philiphaugh 13 September 1645, the very date Charles arrived in Chester on his way to join him. Montrose escaped to the Continent but returned to raise forces for Charles II who subsequently disowned him. In 1650 he landed at Caithness but collected few followers. His force was dispersed at Carbisdale, on 27 April. Abandoning the Star of the Garter which he had recently received Montrose took to the moors and finally sought refuge in the house of Neil Macleod, Laird of Assynt, who betrayed him. He was taken to Edinburgh and executed with barbarity in the High Street, 21 May 1650, walking to his death with proud dignity.

William Cavendish, Earl of Newcastle (1592–1676)

Prominent at court. Made Earl of Newcastle 1628 and was governor of the Prince of Wales from 1638 to 1641. Led troops against the Scots in the Bishops' Wars. Raised the siege of York in 1642. The following year besieged Leeds. Defeated Lord Fairfax and his son, Sir Thomas, at Adwalton Moor near Bradford, 16 June 1643. Made a Marquis the following year. Made great preparations to defend York in 1644 when it was invested by three armies: the Scots under Lord Leven, the northern army under Fairfax, and the Eastern Association under Manchester. When Rupert marched to the relief of York, the Marquis's lack of co-operation cost the cause the battle. After the Royalist defeat the Marquis observed that he would go to Holland as he could not endure the laughter of the court, whereas Rupert said he would rally his men and continue the struggle. Made Duke of Newcastle in 1665. A man of culture as well as wealth. Died Christmas Day, 1676.

Spencer Compton, Earl of Northampton (1601–43)
Leading Royalist in the midlands. Defeated by Brereton and Sir John Gell at Hopton Heath near Stafford though he took most of the Parliamentary artillery. The Earl was unhorsed but continued fighting until killed. He was succeeded by his son, James Compton, a vigorous brigadier.

James Butler, Twelfth Earl of Ormonde (1610–1688)
Created Marquis in 1642, and first Duke in 1661. Supported Wentworth in Ireland. From 1641 to 1643 he kept the Irish in check and was able to despatch regiments to Chester to serve the King. Made Lord-Lieutenant in 1644. From then until 1646 Ormonde had to face both Catholic rebels and Parliamentarians. He was forced to withdraw from Ireland in 1647 but returned the following year when the Second Civil War broke out. Defeated by Cromwell he retired to France where he was in exile with Charles II. Created Duke, he was again Lord-Lieutenant of Ireland, 1662–1669 and 1677–1684. Died 21 July 1688.

Sir John Owen (1600–1666)
In Irish expeditional 1641–2. Ordered by Charles to form a regiment of foot in September 1642 as a bodyguard to the Prince of Wales. Helped to take Cirencester on his way to join the King. Deputy Governor of Reading. Severely wounded in the neck at capture of Bristol. Was at the first battle of Newbury. Knighted at Oxford, 17 December 1644, and appointed Governor of Conway. Vice-Admiral of North Wales. In February 1645 Maurice appointed him Major-General. Turned Parliamentarians out of Wrexham, and in May on his return, he ejected unceremoniously the Archbishop of York who had restored Conway Castle at his own expense. Was not at Naseby but his regiment under Lieutenant-Colonel R. Burgess was almost wiped out. Defended Conway Castle until 18 November though the town was taken by General Thomas Mytton in August. Headed revolt in spring of 1648 and was captured near Bangor, imprisoned, and condemned to die with Hamilton, Holland and Capell, but was pardoned. Several times imprisoned for plotting, and captured at Winnington Bridge in 1659. He died at home and was buried at Penmorfa Church. His brother, Colonel William Owen, was governor of Harlech, the last Royalist fortress to fall.

Prince Rupert (1619–1682)
Born at Prague, son of Frederick V, Elector Palatine, and Elizabeth, sister of Charles I. Rupert is so colourful a personality that it is difficult to assess him at his real worth. He might appear romantic but his nature was stern and ungracious; he was 'always a soldier'. His softer nature seems to have been reserved for his brother Maurice, the King, and Colonel Will Legge, his constant friend. He learnt soldiering in the Thirty Years War during which he was captured and endured three years' imprisonment. He and Maurice crossed to Newcastle in time to join Charles at Nottingham when the Royal Standard was unfurled. In September at Powick Bridge Rupert gave the first of the wild charges associated with his name. Rupert as General of Horse commanded the right wing at Edgehill. He then captured Brentford and advanced on London but at Turnham Green the Royalists were forced to retire to Oxford. Rupert opened the campaign of 1643 by taking Cirencester which surrendered on 2 February. At Lichfield, which defied the Prince, he fired the first mine of war. The city surrendered to bombardment. Reading was next to fall. Rupert's march took him through Chalgrove Field where John Hampden had his death wound. The Prince's next task was to escort Queen Henrietta Maria to rejoin the King. On 18 July Rupert left Oxford for Bristol which he captured 26 July. He next turned his attention to Gloucester which was invested, but despite more of Rupert's mines, the city held out until relieved by the advance of the Earl of Essex from London. It became a race between the armies which would get to London first. They clashed at the first battle of Newbury. Another of Rupert's charges helped to save the day (20 September). Rupert was made President of Wales. On 11 March 1644 he entered Chester where he inspected the mud walls which had been erected outside the ancient ramparts. He left Chester for Newark which he relieved on 21st. After recruiting, he set off on his march through Lancashire, taking Wigan and Liverpool and relieving Lathom House on the march which ended at Marston Moor, 2 July. The defeated Prince, undaunted, recruited between Chester and Shrewsbury, staying awhile at Ruthin Castle. In 1645, by this time generalissimo, he captured Leicester and embarked on the campaign which ended disastrously for the King at Naseby. Rupert went into garrison at Bristol which was captured by Fairfax. His negotiations saved his army (and weapons except firearms). He was, however, censured by the King and exiled, suffering a shoulder wound during an encounter with Parliamentarian forces before embarking for France, where he was made a Maréchal de Camp. When the Second Civil War broke out Rupert took to the sea (as did Maurice) and collected a small Royalist fleet. Off the Irish coast and in the Mediterranean they preyed on British ships until Blake captured most of the Royalist ships at Malaga in 1650. Rupert then sailed for the West Indies and built up another squadron. A gale in 1652 sank the *Constant Reformation*, the ship holding all his plunder, and soon after another storm sank the *Honest Seaman*, with all hands, including his beloved brother Maurice. Broken in spirit Rupert returned to France and went into retirement, devoting his time to art and science. At the Restoration he returned to England but lived a retired life save when he commanded a fleet in the third Dutch War. He founded the Hudson's

Bay Company. After a short illness he died in November 1682 and was buried in Westminster Abbey.

Henry, Lord Wilmot (1612–58)
M.P. Wounded at Powick Bridge. Followed Rupert in Edgehill charge. Stormed Marlborough. Made Lieut-General. With Hopton and Prince Maurice later gained Roundway Down 13 July, 1643. Wounded at Cropredy Bridge and temporarily captured. Helped to relieve York. Charles later dismissed him for contemptuous language.

PARLIAMENTARIAN

Robert Blake (1599–1657)
Son of a Bridgwater merchant. Educated at Oxford. Travelled extensively, visiting India, Morocco and the Netherlands. In 1640 became M.P. for Bridgwater. Distinguished himself by his stubborn defence of Bristol, Lyme and by holding Taunton for over a year. After the King's execution he was appointed a General-at-Sea and revealed latent genius. Driving Rupert's fleet from Irish Coast, he sailed up the Tagus, and finally shattered the Royalist ships at Malaga. Captured Portuguese treasure ships; destroyed a French squadron on its way to relieve Dunkirk. Forced Royalists from Scilly Isles. Won several victories against Dutch. Attacked Tunisian corsairs and burnt their fleet. His greatest exploit was to capture Santa Cruz and annihilate the Spanish treasure fleet. Worn out, he sailed for home but died within sight of the Devon cliffs. Buried in Westminster Abbey, his body was exhumed and re-buried in St. Margaret's churchyard.

Sir William Brereton, B.T., (1604–61)
Parliamentary Commander - in - Chief for Cheshire, Shropshire and Staffordshire, M.P. for Cheshire. Family home, Handforth. A cultured scholar who had travelled on the Continent he was a leading man in the county. At the outset of the war he endeavoured to recruit for Parliament in the City where the mayor ordered his drum to be slashed. Brereton established his headquarters at Nantwich which was surrounded by a mud wall hastily constructed. Following the King's visit to Chester Brereton's town house was ransacked which probably accounted for the severity which characterised his protracted siege. His first assault was in July 1643. In November he collaborated with Sir Thomas Myddelton in invading Wales and taking the castles of Hawarden and Flint before the arrival of troops from Ireland forced him to retreat. When Nantwich was attacked in January 1644 he joined with Sir Thomas Fairfax in defeating the Royalists under Lord Byron. After Marston Moor he marched to the relief of Montgomery Castle and, in company with Sir Thomas Myddelton and Sir John Meldrum, won the battle of Montgomery in September 1644. Following the Parliamentary victory at Rowton Heath, Brereton (though no longer officially Commander-in-Chief on account of the Self-Denying Ordinance) continued to be the nominal leader and forced Byron to surrender Chester (3 February 1646). With Colonel Birch and Colonel Morgan he received the surrender of Lord Astley at Stow-on-the-Wold soon after. Brereton forsook Chester to spend his last years in the sequestrated palace of the Archbishop of Canterbury at Croydon where he died in April 1661, his body being brought back to Handforth for burial.

Oliver Cromwell (1599–1658)
The outstanding figure of his time. Traced his ancestry from Thomas Cromwell, Earl of Essex, Henry VIII's minister whose sister married Morgan Williams of Glamorgan. Their eldest son (Sir) Richard was given Hinchinbroke, Huntingdon. 'I was', said Oliver, 'by birth a gentleman.' He refused to take out knighthood in 1630, and was fined £10. A Puritan, he was averse to ritual as savouring of Romanism. Entered public life as M.P. for Huntingdon in 1628 but soon returned to private life and was not seen in the House until the Short Parliament of 1640, in company with other Puritans such as his cousin, John Hampden, and John Pym. Took the anti-prelatical side when the Grand Remonstrance was carried. His quick grasp of military matters seems to be due to astute discernment and practical application. He informed Hampden that Parliament would never defeat gentlemen with an army of old retainers and tapsters. He set about raising a force of disciplined men of good character who were inspired by religious conviction. His troops of horse increased to ten and finally became a regiment. From being its colonel he became Lieutenant-General in the Eastern Association. Was wounded at Marston Moor where Rupert termed him 'Ironside'—a name subsequently applied to his magnificent regiment. Under the Self-Denying Ordinance he relinquished his rank and Sir Thomas Fairfax was chosen Commander-in-Chief of the New Model Army. After the Royalists sacked Leicester Cromwell was recalled by Parliament and appointed Lieutenant-General of the Horse, arriving at the head of 600 men in time to ensure the defeat of the King at Naseby. Cromwell was sent to clear Wiltshire and Hampshire, and captured Devizes, Winchester, Basing House, and then joined Fairfax before Exeter, finally being at the surrender of Oxford. He returned to Parliamentary duties. In 1646 his daughter Bridget married his chief supporter, Henry Ireton, and another daughter, Elizabeth became wife of John Claypole. The Second Civil War was started by the revolt of Colonel John Poyer in Pembroke and Cromwell was sent to recapture the place—a task which tested his tenacity. As a

Scottish Army under the Duke of Hamilton threatened an invasion Cromwell made a rapid march across to Northampton, took the invaders by surprise on the flank and scattered them at Preston (August 1648). In November the army sent Parliament a 'Remonstrance' demanding punishment of the King as 'the grand author of all their troubles'. Charles was imprisoned but continued to scheme secretly with the Scots. Cromwell (observes Sir Charles Firth) doubted the policy of the King's trial and condemnation if any other satisfactory solution could be devised, but 'the King preferred to part with his life rather than with his regal power'. After the King's execution the monarchy was abolished. Charles, Prince of Wales, in exile was accepted by the Royalists as the new King. When Fairfax resigned as Commander-in-Chief the post was conferred on Cromwell who defeated the Scots at Dunbar (23 September 1650) and at Worcester (exactly a year after) he defeated Charles of Oak Tree fame, his 'final mercy' as Oliver termed it. His health was failing but in 1653 he assumed the role of Lord Protector which he held until his death in 1658 on the anniversary of Dunbar and Worcester. He was buried with great pomp in Westminster Abbey, but after the Restoration was exhumed and his body hanged on Tyburn gallows.

Robert Devereux, third Earl of Essex, (1591–1646)
Parliamentary Commander-in-Chief at outset of the Civil War when his illustrious name was more conspicuous than his ability. In 1604 he regained the title his father had lost by his rebellion against Queen Elizabeth. Chosen by James I as a companion for Prince Henry. Served in the Thirty Years War without distinction. In 1625 he participated in the unfortunate expedition against Cadiz, and in 1639 held a command in Charles's campaign against the Covenanters. Appointed commander by the Parliament at the outbreak of the Civil War he marched the London trained bands out to defend the city which was threatened by the King. This terminated at Edgehill on 23 October which found Essex facing the city he was supposed to defend and the King with his back to the capital he was proposing to capture. Essex's best achievement was his march which dispersed the Royalist forces besieging Gloucester. He commanded at the first battle of Newbury, 20 September 1643. The King, short of powder, fell back on Oxford and Essex was able to carry the survivors of the ill-managed fight safely to London. He led the army to Cornwall. Having been defeated at Lostwithiel in August 1644, he escaped in a fishing-boat leaving the army to its fate. He resigned his position when the Self-Denying Ordinance was passed the following year and died 14 September, 1646.

Sir Thomas (later third Lord) Fairfax (1612–1671)
Son of Ferdinando, second Lord Fairfax, was born at Denton, Yorkshire, and saw service in the Netherlands and also against the Scots. His father was among the King's opponents and Thomas operated with him at first but soon showed the greater enterprise. He was moderate and, according to Richard Baxter, 'religious, faithful and valiant.' Both Lord Fairfax and Sir Thomas were at Marston Moor. Their two regiments were scattered by Goring's fiery charge on the Royalist left wing. Lord Fairfax fled towards Hull, but Sir Thomas, though wounded, tore the distinguishing badge from his hat and crossed to assist the Earl of Manchester's force. On the passing of the Self-Denying Ordinance, Sir Thomas was chosen Commander-in-Chief for Parliament. He was 32 years old. After gaining the battle of Naseby (14 June 1645), followed by his successful campaign in the West, he became a popular hero, but was already breaking from the extremists. In the Second Civil War he crushed the revolt in the south-east and after a long siege captured Colchester, which fell on 28 August. A Council of War ordered the execution of two gallant Cavaliers captured, Sir Charles Lucas and Sir George Lisle. Contrary to Fairfax's wishes they were shot. He refused to sit in judgment on the King. In 1650, being reluctant to lead a campaign against the Presbyterian Scots (the religion he favoured) the high command was given to Cromwell. Lord Fairfax retired and was voted a pension of £5,000 a year. He helped Monk to bring about the Restoration. Though elected M.P. for Yorkshire, he took no further part in public affairs.

Charles Fleetwood (1618–1692)
Son of Sir Miles Fleetwood. Educated Gray's Inn. Joined Parliamentary army in 1642. As a captain of horse wounded at Newbury. Raised his own regiment which became part of the New Model. Extreme Puritan. In 1647 resisted the order to go to Ireland or disband. Elected M.P. for Marlborough. Married Bridget, widow of Henry Ireton. He fought at Dunbar and Worcester, succeeded Ireton as Commander-in-Chief in Ireland. Did not join Monk at the Restoration period.

Colonel John Hampden (1594–1643)
Cousin of Cromwell. M.P. of outstanding ability yet content to remain subordinate. In 1635 attracted attention by refusing to pay Ship Money. One of the Five Members. Signed Grand Remonstrance. Raised a regiment of foot (Greencoats) and fought at Edgehill and Brentford and took part in the relief of Coventry and the siege of Reading. Encountered Rupert at Chalgrove Field, receiving a dangerous wound from which he died at Thame on 24 June.

Major-General Thomas Harrison (1616–1660)
Capable soldier but a fanatical believer in the 'second coming' of Christ which he believed victory would ensure. Born in Newcastle-under-

Lyme, son of a butcher, apprenticed clerk to an attorney, he enlisted in Essex's bodyguard when war broke out. Was at Edgehill. Captain of Horse under Fleetwood in 1644 he served as Major at Marston Moor and Naseby. Was conspicuous at Langport, 'as though he had been in a rapture'. Commanded a regiment of horse. Wished to abolish House of Lords and to prosecute the King. With Lambert before Preston, he received several wounds. He was in charge of the cavalry guard which conducted Charles to Hurst Castle and Commissioner for Propagation of the Gospel in Wales. Took command in London, 1650, when Cromwell marched to Scotland. Fought at Worcester. Figured in the removal of the Mace incident in 1653. His name is on Charles' death warrant. At the Restoration he would neither acknowledge Charles II nor flee and was executed as a regicide, 13 October 1660.

Henry Ireton (1611–1651)
Born at Attenborough, of an ancient Nottingham family. A young man of university and legal training he became at the outbreak of war, Captain of one of Cromwell's troops of horse. Promoted colonel he fought at Marston Moor and the second battle of Newbury. At Naseby, as Commissary-General he commanded the Parliamentary horse on the left wing, and when charged by Rupert was wounded and temporarily taken prisoner. That year, 1645, he entered Parliament as Member for Appleby and drafted the Heads of the Proposals. He then returned to military affairs, and about this time married Cromwell's eldest daughter Bridget. Ireton shared the religious faith of his father-in-law and strove for religious liberty. In 1647 he laboured to mollify the discontented soldiers, favouring discussion to force. When an agreement between King and Parliament failed, Ireton was one who signed the Royal death warrant. Ireton followed Cromwell to Ireland and during 1650 he with General Ludlow undertook most of the fighting. Left as Lord Deputy he captured Waterford and Limerick but died of the plague on 26 November 1651. He was buried in Westminster Abbey but at the Restoration his body was exhumed and hanged on Tyburn gallows.

Major-General 'Honest John' Lambert (1619–1684)
Born at Carlton, Yorkshire. Educated Trinity College, Cambridge. Studied law at one of the Inns of Court. Captain in horse regiment of Sir Thomas Fairfax. A born soldier he had a cavalry regiment of his own by the end of 1643 and subsequently was colonel of a foot regiment as well. Served under Fairfax at the relief of Nantwich, and, returning to Yorkshire captured Selby from Colonel John Belasyse, a relative of Lambert's wife. Served at Marston Moor under Fairfax, who the following January appointed him Commissary-General of the Northern Army in the New Model Army. After Naseby (where he was not engaged in the actual battle) he participated in the pursuit and followed Fairfax to the West where (with Ireton) he negotiated the surrender of Hopton's army. He also helped to negotiate the surrender of Oxford (June 1646) and was temporarily appointed Governor where he prevented damage being done to the buildings. Made Major-General in 1647, by 28 he ranked as the third most important Parliamentarian after Cromwell and Fairfax. Was one of the signatories of the army's 'Remonstrance' presented to Parliament that year. In the Second Civil War he played a prominent part in the north and helped Cromwell to win the Preston campaign. He recaptured Pontefract Castle, and played a major part in the victory at Dunbar. The following year when Charles II marched south to Worcester, Lambert followed down the eastern flank, covering 200 miles in 10 days. By repairing the bridge at Upton and moving 11,000 men to the river's west bank, he contributed to the defeat of the Scottish invaders. Though Lambert several times declined to receive sums voted him by Parliament he was sufficiently wealthy (and ambitious) to buy Wimbledon Palace where he and his charming wife Frances dwelt in state. The Lord Protector created him one of his Lords. Lambert was largely responsible for the 'Instrument of Government' which created Cromwell Lord Protector. He strove unsuccessfully to resist the Restoration, was captured, imprisoned in the Tower, escaped, but after his recapture he was incarcerated in Castle Cornet, Guernsey in 1662. He died a captive on Drake's Island, 1684, and was buried in St. Andrew's Church, Plymouth on 28 March.

Major-General Roland Laugharne
Outstanding Parliamentarian in South Wales. His captures included Haverfordwest, Tenby and Carmarthern. He also helped 'Admiral' Richard Swanley to take the fort at the Pill in Milford Haven. The arrival of General Charles Gerard robbed Laugharne of many of his gains but eventually he defeated the Royalists at Colby Moor. He had charge of the operations against Aberystwyth though the actual siege was conducted by his deputy Colonel Rice Powell. In the Second Civil War Laugharne joined Colonel Poyer and Colonel Rice Powell who captured Pembroke Castle for the King. Colonel Thomas Horton defeated and scattered the Royalists at St. Fagans, 8 May 1648. Laugharne, Powell and Poyer were later taken in Pembroke and sentenced to be shot. But the prisoners were allowed to draw lots as to which should be executed and the lot fell on Poyer. Laugharne went overseas.

Edmund Ludlow (1617–1693)
A Wiltshire man of good education and a republican, he left a valuable autobiography. From being a Colonel he was made Lieutenant-General of Horse in Ireland in succession to Colonel Michael Jones, dead of fever. He was then 33. Refused to acknowledge Protectorate and plotted against Cromwell. Fled to Vevey in

Switzerland but after the 'Glorious Revolution' (1688) he returned to England. But at 71 he was still a menace and his arrest was ordered whereupon he escaped and returned to Vevey where he died.

Edward Montagu, second Earl of Manchester (1602–1671)

A prominent member of the 'popular' party in the House of Lords, his name was added to the names of the five members Charles impeached for treason in 1642. He was nominally in command at Marston Moor and won the second battle of Newbury, but his dilatory conduct in the pursuit irritated Cromwell, and may have sown the seed for the Self-Denying Ordinance which deprived him and other members of their military rank. Helped to bring about the Restoration and was made K.G. in 1661.

Sir Thomas Myddelton, KT., (1586–1666)

Admitted Gray's Inn. Received Chirk Castle for wedding present. Knighted 1617. M.P. Weymouth, 1624, Denbigh County 1625, Long Parliament 1640 until retirement in 1648. Having sent a 'menacing' letter to constituents urging them to support Parliament in December, 1642, the irate King ordered Colonel Robert Ellice to capture Chirk castle and appropriate the plate to form a regiment of foot. Myddelton was commissioned Sergeant-Major-General of the Parliament for North Wales, and 'sub-general' to Sir William Brereton whom he joined at Nantwich in August with a mixed force which included seven great guns. Myddelton and Brereton in November rushed Holt bridge and captured Wrexham, Hawarden and Flint but soon had to retire. Myddelton helped in the capture of Oswestry, took Royalist horse at Welshpool, occupied Montgomery Castle and helped to defeat Byron there in September 1644, then captured Red Castle (Powis). He took Ruthin town (but not castle) and made an unsuccessful attempt to recapture Chirk Castle at Christmas. The Self-Denying Ordinance terminated his commission. By the Second Civil War his moderate views rendered him suspect. In 1659 he joined Booth's Rebellion and proclaimed Charles II king at Wrexham. Defeated at Winnington Bridge, and his home again captured, he went into hiding until the Restoration. His eldest son, also Sir Thomas, was created a baronet. Old Sir Thomas declined any honours but accepted a beautiful inlay cabinet, still in use today. It is estimated that his losses and damage to his estate totalled £85,000.

Major-General Thomas Mytton (1597–1656)

From Halston, he was the leading Parliamentarian in Shropshire. First attracted attention when he defended Wem with 300 men against Capel's 4,000 Royalists. In January 1644 Mytton surprised and captured at Ellesmere Sir Nicholas Byron, Governor of Chester, and Sir Richard Willis. Mytton aided the Earl of Denbigh to capture Oswestry in June 1644. In Montgomery Castle in September 1644 while the battle was fought nearby he caught Sir William Vaughan, Governor of Shrawardine Castle, Shropshire, and used him as hostage to persuade the garrison to surrender; but under pretence of arranging a parley Vaughan (according to Roland Phillips) entered his castle and refused to submit. After the Self-Denying Ordinance Mytton succeeded Sir Thomas Myddelton as commander in North Wales. (Their wives were sisters). Assisted in attack on Chester and was largely responsible for Vaughan's defeat on Denbigh Green. Captured all Royalist castles in North Wales. In Second Civil War crushed the Anglesey revolt at the Battle of Beaumaris.

Major-General Philip Skippon (d. 1660)

Major-General of Foot. A veteran of the Thirty Years War where he was wounded. Was from the first the idol of the London Trained Bands. Fought at Newbury. After Lostwithiel campaign when Essex deserted his army Skippon took command and arranged terms of surrender. Was at Naseby. 'Stout Skippon hath a wound,' wrote Macaulay in his Naseby poem. In 1647 Skippon took charge when the Scots handed over the king.

Sir William Waller (1597–1668)

Though nicknamed 'William the Conqueror' experienced several notable defeats. The son of a Lieutenant of Dover Castle, he served in the Venetian army and the Thirty Years War. He and Sir Ralph Hopton were comrades-in-arms under Rich's command, and maintained the friendship despite the Civil War. Waller was knighted by James I in 1622. At the outbreak of war he was made a Parliamentary Colonel of Horse to serve in the West Country where the Royalist leader was Sir Ralph Hopton. Waller's letter to Hopton is one of the most moving writings of the war. Protesting that his affections were unchangeable, Waller added that he detested 'this war without an Enemie'. 'Wee are both upon the stage and must act those parts that are assigned to us in this Tragedy: Lett us do it in a way of honor, and without personal annimosities, whatsoever the issue be.' The following month Hopton defeated Waller at Lansdown (5 July). At Roundway Down on 13 July Waller was again defeated by the combined efforts of Hopton, Lord Wilmot and Sir John Byron who arrived in time to force the issue. Waller escaped to Bristol. London citizens raised for him an army with which he besieged Basing House, and captured Arundel. Hopton, who recovered from his wound, was defeated by Waller at Cheriton (29 March 1644). Waller sustained another defeat at Cropredy Bridge three months later. A Member of Parliament, it was his suggestion that a standing army was needed that produced the 'New Model', and turned the tide of war. He retired under the Self-Denying Ordinance. As a Presbyterian he would not have appreciated the growing power of the Independents. Later he worked for the Restoration.

COLOURS & HERALDRY

by Brigadier Peter Young

'... and indeed a greater Act of Cowardice cannot be found, than to suffer the Colours to be lost.' (*Thomas Venn*)

Until at least as late as the reign of King James II, every troop of Horse and company of Foot or Dragoons had its own standard, colour or guidon. Parliamentarian and Cavalier troops both followed the same system. It must be emphasised that purely regimental colours were a later development.

The Role of the Colours
The colours were of considerable importance because, whether in action or in quarters, they marked the headquarters of the troop or company. When the regiment dismissed at night, each company lodged its colours with some ceremony at the house where officers were billeted. In the days when practically all the N.C.O.s and men were unlettered, it was important to emphasise that the captain's quarter was the alarm post in case of a surprise, and the parade ground at the beginning of each day's work. Though larger than the colours now in use, those of the foot being of taffeta were light, and it was the duty of the ensign who bore them to flourish them in an elaborate fashion when on the march. By the Law of Arms, a troop or company that lost its colour might not bear a new one until it had taken one from the enemy in action. When, as frequently happened, a fortress or even an army was compelled to surrender, the defeated party in suing for terms invariably demanded that they be allowed to march away with their colours. One finds examples of regiments surrendering their firearms but persuading their captors to leave them their standards.

Above: A reconstruction of 'The Banner Royall'.

On the other hand, captured colours made good trophies, and officers charged with taking them to the King were frequently rewarded with a knighthood; equally, the fortunate messenger to London after a Parliamentarian victory, could usually expect a handsome monetary reward.

The task of carrying the colours was not altogether enviable. At the beginning of a pitched battle, they made a fair mark for the enemy cannon. In a mêlée, both sides strove lustily to seize the colours of the opposite party, and there is some evidence that standard-bearers were selected from among the the stoutest hearted and most athletic gentlemen available. From the eighteenth century when colours were regimental, the ensigns were the junior officers, often mere boys, but this does not seem to have been the case in Stuart times.

The Battle of Cropredy Bridge affords two examples of the way in which men fought for these coveted trophies. Captain Boswell had three of his fingers cut off, 'yet found a hand to bring off one of the Rebels colours. Cornet Brook of Sir William Boteler's regiment was sore hurt but not before he had killed a rebel cannonier with his Cornet's staff as he was in the act of firing a gun'. The Prince of Wales' troop lost its cornet at Hopton Heath, but Major Thomas Daniel took one from the Parliamentarians at Chalgrove Field three months later and restored the troop's honour. The value of these trophies is emphasied by the fact that Parliamentarian soldiers who took colours at Marston Moor (1644) and Dunbar (1650) were rewarded with ten shillings a piece—no mean sum in those days.

Horse
Cavalry standards measured approximately 2ft by 2ft and were fringed. They were generally made of painted taffeta, though the standards of the colonel's troop were usually of plain damask without any device. Sometimes the standards were adorned with heraldic devices derived from the arms of the troop commander. More often they bore some kind of political slogan. For example, among the Royalist standards taken at Marston Moor was one described as 'A yellow cornet, and in the middle a sleeping Lyon, at whose breech lyeth snatching a mastife Dog, with word as it were preceeding from his mouth, Kimbolton, and at his feet little beagles, and before their mouthes, Pym, Pym, Pym, with these words preceeding from his mouth, Quosque tandem abutere patientia nostra? that is, how long will (sic) you abuse our patience?'. Examples from the Parliamentarian side show a picture of an armed soldier with his sword drawn, threatening a kneeling bishop. Out of the soldier's mouth comes the caption 'Visne episcopari' ('do you want to be a bishop?') and out of the bishop's mouth the words 'Nolo, nolo' ('no, no').

In 1645 Lord Charles Gerard's Lifeguard had a standard with a sphere painted on it and the motto 'At all that's round'.

Sometimes the device was not political but merely referred to the status of employment of its owner. King Charles I's Lifeguard, for example, bore a lion passant, crowned *or* with 'Dieu et mon Droit,' and in 1644 Lord Hopton as General of the Artillery had for his Lifeguard a standard *gules* bearing the device of a cannon discharging *or*, and the motto 'Et sacris compescuit ignibus ignes' ('He extinguishes fires with sacred fires').

Others showed their loyalty to King and religion with mottoes such as 'Deo et Caesari' ("To God and Caesar') borne by Sir Edward Widdrington's troop, and 'In hoc signo vinces' ('In this sign conquer'), the device of Lieutenant-Colonel Henry Constable.

On the Parliamentarian side, as we have seen, the

Above: The King's Lifeguard of Foot, Captain. Left, St. George's Cross; right, the Crown and the Lion are Gold, the motto black on white, the field red.

standards mostly enshrined religious and political ideas. Sir Arthur Hesilrige bore a standard portraying an anchor, hanging as it were from a cloud, and the motto 'Only in Heaven' written beneath. The Earl of Essex's Lifeguard bore a colour with the motto 'Cave, Adsum!' ('Beware, I am here!'). This the Cavaliers unkindly interpreted as referring to their ignominious flight in their first action at Powick Bridge (23 September, 1642).

The trumpets had little banners which seem to have been the same as the standards of the troop. This was certainly so in the case of the Royalist captain, Sir Richard Astley, Bt., whose monument at Patshull Church shows that he wore the cinquefoil of his house on his standard, his trumpet banner and the caparison of his charger.

There are still two Cavalier standards of the Civil War period preserved in the church at Bromsberrow.

Foot
The colours were of painted taffeta and measured $6\frac{1}{2}$ft × $6\frac{1}{2}$ft.

Captain Thomas Venn describes the protocol: 'The Colonel's Colours in the first place is of a pure and clean colour, without any mixture. The Lieutenant Colonels only with Saint George's Armes in the

Above: The King's Lifeguard of Foot, First Captain's Colour. Left, St. George's Cross; right, Tudor Rose, crowned on a red field.

upper corner next the staff, the Major's the same, but in the lower and outmost corner with a little stream Blazant, and every Captain with Saint George's Armes alone, but with so many spots or several Devices as pertain to the dignity of their respective places.'

Some regiments, including the King's Lifeguard of Foot and Prince Rupert's Bluecoats, had rather more elaborate colours which did not conform to this system.

The colours used all had their own significance and, as in heraldry, it was wrong to put metal on a metal.

Yellow (Gold): 'honour, or height of Spirit'.

White (Silver): 'signifieth Innocencie, or purity of conscience, Truth, and upright integrity without blemish'.

Black: 'signifieth Wisdome, and sobriety, together with a severe correction of too much Ambition, being mixed with Yellow, or with too much belief or lenity being mixed with White'.

Blue: 'Faith, constancy or truth in affection'.

Red: 'Justice, or Noble worthy Anger in defence of Religion or the oppressed'.

Green: 'good hope, or the accomplishment of holy and honourable actions'.

Purple: 'fortitude with discretion, or a most true discharge of any trust reposed'.

Tunnis or Tawny: 'signifieth merit, or desert, and a foe to Ingratitude'.

Ermine: 'only a rich Furr, with curious spots, signifieth Religion, or holiness, and that all names are not divine objects'.

Although colonels used devices from their arms to differentiate the various companies, it was not difficult to confuse a Parliamentarian for a Royalist colour. In 1642 Major Will Legge and in 1644 Lieutenant Colonel Frank Butler fell into the hands of Parliamentarians, simply because they mistook a regiment of the other side for one of their own. Examples of the spots or devices used were gold lions on the blue colours of the Earl of Stamford's regiment (Parliamentarian), white cinquefoils on the blue colours of Sir Edward Stradling's regiment and dogs on the yellow (gold) colours of Colonel Talbot; these last two being Royalist.

Firth gives an interesting example of Parliamentarian colours ordered by Colonel Charles Fairfax in 1650 when he was given a regiment of foot to serve against the Scots. He chose the colours of his nephew, Lord Fairfax, blue and white, and asked a friend in London to order the colours. 'All the ten flags were to be made "of the best taffaty of the deepest blue that can be gotten". His own was to be "at least two yards square" and to bear upon it "within a well-wrought round, these two words one under the other, 'Fideliter, Faeliciter,'". The lieutenant-colonel's flag was likewise to be blue, but with the red cross of England in one corner, and the the major's "blue with the red cross and white streaks". Finally, the eldest captain and the rest of the captains according to seniority were to be distinguished by one or more white mullets (or stars) in a blue field.

Dragoons

Dragoons were mounted infantry and almost always fought on foot, travelling on their nags or cobbs from place to place, but not usually charging like the Horse. The only example of Dragoons making a cavalry charge at this period was Colonel John Okey's regiment of the New Model Army in the last phase of the Battle of Naseby. The guidons of the dragoon company were much the same size as cavalry standards and these too were fringed, but had a rounded swallowtail on the side furthest from the pole. The system for differentiating the various companies followed the infantry rather than the cavalry pattern.

COAT COLOURS

During the English Civil War no true system of uniform colouring was followed until the appearance of the New Model Army in their red coats. Regiments were raised and very often financed by their colonels, who alone decided what colour coats they should wear. The following list does not set out to be definitive, but simply to give the reader some idea of the regimental coat colours worn on either side— thereby illustrating how difficult it must have been to tell one side from the other. (As a general rule, coat colours were usually the same colour as the field of the regiment's standards.)

Royalist
The King's Lifeguard: red
The Queen's Regiment of Foot: red
Prince Rupert's Lifeguard: blue
Marquess of Newcastle: white
Charles Gerard: blue
Earl of Northampton: green
Earl of Lindsey: red
Lord Hopton: blue
Lord Percy: white
Sir Henry Bard: grey
Henry Tillier: green
Robert Broughton: green
Sir William Saville: red

Parliament
Earl of Essex: orange
John Hampden: green
Sir John Merrick: grey
Earl of Stamford: blue
Lord Brooke: purple
Lord Robartes: red
Sir Henry Cholmley: blue
Denzil Holles: red
Thomas Grantham: russet
Sir William Constable: blue
Thomas Ballard: grey
Lord Feilding: grey

MILITARY *costume*

by Lieutenant-Colonel J. B. R. Nicholson

*'The daubing of a coat with lace
of sundry colours, as some do use them,
I do neither take to be soldierlike
nor profitable for the coat.'
(John Malet, 1643)*

Before discussing the costume of this period in detail it might be as well to dismiss the common misconception that all cavaliers were dressy alcoholics solely preoccupied with wine, women and song, and that all parliamentarians were dismal, bible thumping, psalm singing religious maniacs wearing horizontally striped sleeves. Both types were undoubtedly to be found, but in very limited numbers. The majority of the inhabitants of these islands were not readily distinguishable in their dress for their political sympathies.

Whilst it is possible to establish that certain fashions came into use at certain approximate dates this is by no means to assert that they were universally adopted. Communications were slow and fashions changed less rapidly than today when the clothing trade survives only on the principle of immediate obsolescence. Good clothes were expensive and not lightly discarded. Furthermore, elderly and middle-aged persons, as also the more conservative, were prone to adhere to the fashions of their youth both in clothes and hairstyles, having, even to the youth of their own time, an old-fashioned appearance. The same might be said of weapons and armour during a period when every barn and attic would have been scoured for serviceable items, and doubtless many a piece of antique pattern was pressed into service. To further complicate the picture, doubtless many who had travelled or soldiered abroad would have adopted the style of costume to which they had become accustomed.

In general the period was noticeable for the rapid disappearance of the stiff, almost hieratic appearance of the two previous reigns, in the decline of padding, starched ruffs and farthingales. This resulted in a softer, more flowing line. The slashing of sleeves and doublets was more restrained and decoration less elaborate, and effect was achieved in general more by texture and colour. Amongst the more sober nonconformists the garments were of the simpler styles in quiet colours, but it should be remembered that all who supported Parliament were not Puritans; nor indeed could all sober persons find it in their conscience to oppose their lawful King.

Hair
There was a tendency for hair to lengthen during the period and fashionables would be in the van, but many wore short hair for a variety of reasons. Short hair might be worn by

the old-fashioned or by anyone who found long hair troublesome to manage or considered it too 'worldly'. The hygenic disadvantages of long hair were to lead to the widespread use of wigs from about 1660 until the early nineteenth century.

Long hair was sometimes worn with a fringe across the forehead, or brushed back as shown in portraits of the King, and shoulder-length hair was sometimes curled inwards at the bottom in what is referred to as 'page boy' style. Sometimes lovelocks were worn, plaited or tied with ribbon. The full beard was still popular although in general the beard tended to diminish throughout the period, assuming the well known Van Dyck shape. It had almost disappeared by the end of the century. The moustache, universally worn, full and often brushed up in 'Laughing Cavalier' style, also diminished to the hair line of Charles II, and was almost extinct by the end of the century. (It may be observed that in the popular mind, that inexhaustable fund of misconceptions, the position was the reverse of today, when short back and sides tends to be politically equated with the Right, and long hair with the Left.)

Linen
Shirts were cut very full in the body and sleeves, and were often visible through the slashes with which doublets were plentifully ventilated. Neck linen was worn in a variety of styles from the old-fashioned starched ruff

A mid-seventeenth century doublet, richly made, with button-up fastening, and shown with a lavish lace collar. (Victoria & Albert Museum.)

favoured by the elderly, the conservative, and professional men, to the wide collar, often laced with deep scallops. The tasselled tie-string is often visible in portraits. Towards the end of the period the collar generally shrank in size and the lace became less elaborate. In any case the rich lace was always the perquisite of the well-to-do; the commonest form was a simple collar, best described as an unstarched Eton collar.

At the wrist linen bands were worn which might either fall downwards over the back of the hand, or be turned back over the cuff. When laced this often matched that used on the collar.

Headgear

The normal headgear was the broad-brimmed hat. This was worn by both men and women, and could be quite plain with simple band or cord, or ornamented with a more or less elaborate hat band, plus buckles and feathers in such colours and quantity as pleased the owner. A sort of fisherman's cap was also worn, and, much favoured by dragoons, something called a Montero cap. Of this latter little seems to be known, but it appears to have had some sort of resemblance to a jockey cap, possibly of the type worn by footmen or runners in the Blenheim tapestries of a later date.

Body Garments

By the time the Civil War broke out the doublet with six-panelled skirts attached by laces was already going out of fashion, although it was still

Fashionable cavaliers, showing the wear of slashed sleeves, wide laced collars and cuffs, broad-brimmed hats, extravagantly decorated with buckles and plumes. The doublet and breeches are well ornamented with lace and buttons, and the large turned-down boots reveal boot-hose just below the knee. They are also wearing spurs and 'butterfly' guard leathers. Voluminous cloaks are here shown slung over the left shoulder, and both are wearing their rapiers in decorated baldrics. (Victoria & Albert Museum.)

widely used. It was made with wings on the shoulders and sleeves might be fairly tight or loose and paned or slashed to the wrist or elbow. The neck had a low collar, upright and fastened in front. The body might have as many as eight vertical slashes on the breast and as many on the back, and the sleeves were also sometimes slashed at the back from top to bottom. The quantity of lace and embroidery and the materials used were dictated by personal choice and size of purse, and varied from extreme richness to sober plainness. At times buttons were used in extravagant profusion as a form of decoration. It seems probable that the panels of the skirts were sewn to the top, and that the points or lacing ribbons were by now purely decorative and serving no useful purpose. Throughout our period there was a tendency to shorten and straighten the waist line and to lengthen the skirts which were cut more horizontally at the bottom. It was common to leave this type of coat unfastened below the breast. From about 1640 this pattern became very popular; from portraits it is difficult to distinguish waist or skirts, and the cuff is often turned back to show the lining and shirt sleeve to advantage. By the time of the Restoration the jacket had so shrunk that the shirt was visible all round the waistline. It may be noted that the slashes revealed either the shirt or a lining of a contrasting colour.

The buff coat made of stout hide was a garment held in high esteem, and worn not only by military men but also those who liked the military image. The excessive weight of armour required to withstand firearms caused armour to fall into disfavour. In fact within half a century it was to disappear altogether except for fitful use of the breastplate and the gorget, which was to survive in decreasing size as the insignia of an infantry officer until abolished in the nineteenth century. The buff coat was worn either as the sole protection in battle or under armour. It was laced, buttoned or fastened with frogs up the front, and often had sleeves, which might be slashed and made to fasten. If not made with sleeves of leather they were often provided with cloth sleeves, thus rendering a doublet unnecessary. They were usually made with wings on the shoulders which afforded additional protection. Buff coats were sometimes ornamented with gold or silver lace or

The buff coat, worn by most of the cavalry during the Civil War. A simple garment, it was light and comfortable to wear in comparison to armour, and would protect the wearer from all but the heaviest of sword blows. This one is fastened by lace, and there is an interesting overlap of the skirts, which would have counteracted the tendency of a horseman's coat to fly open. Buff coats were also worn with full-length sleeves, sometimes of double thickness. (Victoria & Albert Museum.)

embroidery. As with the doublet, the skirts gradually diminished, the four large panels shrinking to negligible proportions.

Breeches
Breeches came in a variety of patterns. The commonest type were loose, fastened at the knee with a band, often ornamented with lace and buttons up the outer seam, which was sometimes left unfastened for several inches above the knee to reveal a contrasting lining. Alternatively they might be quite close fitting after the style of knee-breeches. Sometimes, as in one of the portraits of Prince Charles, the breeches are almost completely hidden under close-set vertical bands of gold braid. A different style again was open ended (that is, quite loose round the knee) and often finished with loops of lace or braid; from about 1645 loops proliferated round the waistband, down the front, at the knees and even on the outside of the thighs.

Footwear
This period was pre-eminently the age of the boot: the boot was worn not only for equestrian occasions but also about the house and even at balls. Silk stockings, sometimes several pairs at once, were worn by those who could afford them, home-knitted yarn by others. To protect these and the breeches from the rub of the boot, additional boot-hose were worn. These were often edged with lace, and it is this which gave the froth of lace in the boot tops when folded down to form bucket tops. For riding the boots were of course pulled well up. During this period toes grew steadily squarer, and it was fashionable to have the heels and sole edges red. Massive spurs were worn, the guard leathers assuming an exaggerated quatrefoil shape. Simple wooden clogs were often worn with boots and shoes, frequently permanently attached to the soles. (Many of the boots shown in contemporary portraits appear to fit so closely that it remains a mystery how they were ever put on!)

Ordinary leather shoes had loops cut out of the sides and were ornamented with rosettes which gradually gave place to bows of ribbon.

Cloaks and Coats
Short cloaks were now little worn, having given way to medium and long cloaks and cassocks worn with or without collars. They could be worn in a wide variety of fashions—hung over one shoulder, or hung around the neck with the bottom right corner flung over the left shoulder in Spanish style, and so on. Cassocks or coats of varying lengths, the sleeves with heavy cuffs, and often much belaced and ornamented with buttons, had the sleeves slit down the front, fastening with loops and buttons. These garments were frequently worn with the arms thrust through the slits and the sleeves hanging down behind. When the cloak was worn over both shoulders it was normal to wear the lace or linen collar over the cape. Members of Orders of Chivalry wore the badge of the Order embroidered, often very large, on the left breast of the garment for ordinary wear (quite apart from special embroidered robes or uniform for the Order).

Accessories
Amongst the military and those with military pretentions the two main items were the broad military sash—fringed and tied in a great bow over the left hip—and the gorget. The gorget was a piece of neck armour which survived the general disuse of armour to become the insignia of an infantry officer, and as such, in ever diminishing size, it survived as a small gilt crescent, until abolished in the British Army in 1831. The sword was worn either in a waistbelt, as in Elizabethan times or in a shoulder-belt or baldric. These varied from the plainest leather to the richest embroidered materials.

Armour

by Marcus Hinton

'Whereas the defensive arms of horsemen and pikemen are much slighted by some in these times, I would have such know that souldiers ought to go into the field to conquer, and not be killed; and I would have our young gallants to take notice that men wear not armour because they are afraid of danger, but because they would not fear it.' (Monck, Observations*)*

The Civil War was the last major conflict when Englishmen went into battle wearing armour; even so, in the course of the struggle armour was falling into disuse and by the end of the century it had become obsolete. The fundamental reason for this was the improvement of firearms and their wide adoption by European armies through the preceding century.

Armourers had answered the challenge of improved firearms by increasing the thickness and, in consequence, the weight of armour, in order to make it bulletproof, and they had—to a considerable degree—succeeded. Much of the armour of the early seventeenth century was bulletproofed at least against the lighter pistol bullet. The evidence for this still exists in the proofmark, a round dent caused by the deliberate firing of a bullet at close range to test the reliability of manufacture and often seen on breastplates. (These marks have since given rise to interesting and erroneous legends that the original wearers had had close shaves in action.) But as the armourer succeeded in his efforts to make heavy armour that was bulletproof, the soldier became more reluctant to carry the heavy load, despite the reassurance of the proofmark, and hence the gradual fade out of the armoured warrior.

When the Civil War began both the King and Parliament had to form, arm, and equip their armies from scratch. Parliament enjoyed a great advantage in their control of London —which represented the well-equipped Trained Bands, the Tower armoury with its racks of weapons and, most important of all, the City finances which made possible the purchase of more arms and armour. Parliament's good fortune went one stage further, for the military magazine at Hull also fell into their hands. The King, in the first instance, was compelled to rely on the private armouries of his supporters, together with the arms and armour of those trained bands which could be induced, by one means or another, to yield their weapons to more resolute spirits. This was not sufficient, so Charles' redoubtable queen, Henrietta Maria, went to the Continent, there to pawn the Crown jewels and purchase arms, armour, and equipment from the proceeds. Thus Continental armour was used during the English Civil War, supplementing the domestic gear of both sides. And it is important to remember that there was no great difference between the style and amount of armour worn by Cavaliers and Roundheads.

Infantry Armour

Pikemen wore a helmet, breast- and backplates (often with the addition of a metal collar or gorget), and tassets (metal thigh guards) were frequently fastened to the base of the breastplate. The helmet, or pikeman's pot, was a metal cap with a low comb and a wide rim round the edge which

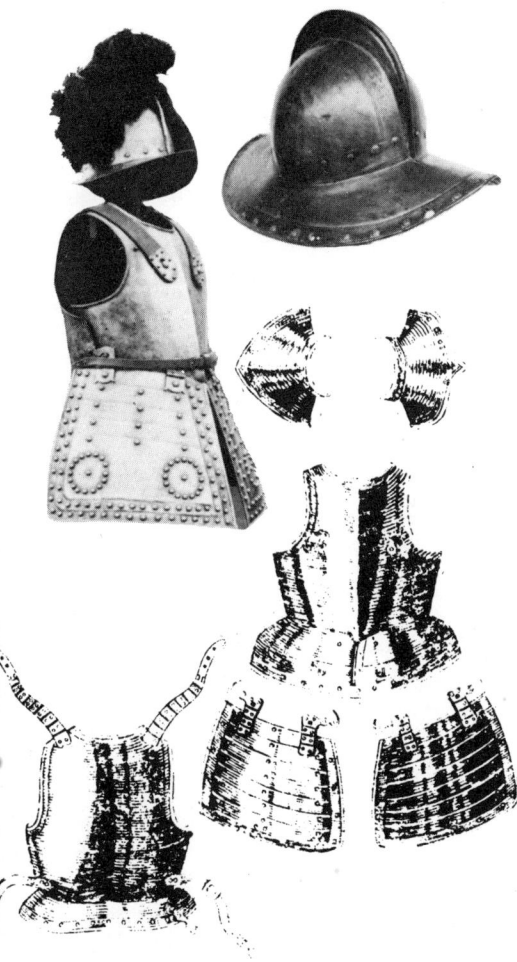

Pikeman's armour, shown strapped together as worn (top), and in its individual parts as shown in a military handbook of 1616.

provided a glancing surface. The pot was constructed in two halves, being joined along the length of the comb by the turning over of the edges. It often had ear flaps which, apart from providing additional protection, were given leather thongs tying under the chin and securing the helmet firmly in place. The metal collar was made in two sections, hinged at the left and fastened on the right by a stud fitting into a keyhole-shaped slot.

The breastplate was shaped with a vertical central ridge, ending with a pointed projection over the wearer's stomach; all edges were turned outwards to deflect an opponent's weapon. The backplate was shaped to the human figure and again had turned edges; on some better quality armour the turned edges were emphasized and given a roped effect. The backplate had two halves of a waistbelt riveted to the sides, which fastened in front around the breastplate. Two wider leather straps were riveted to the top of the backplate. These were the shoulder straps, ending in metal plates with the keyhole-shaped slots to fasten over the metal studs on the breastplate. The shoulder straps were sometimes reinforced with small metal squares to guard against an enemy's sword-cut. The pair of tassets, which reached almost to the knee, were fastened to the base of the breast plate in a variety of ways; some were attached by buckle and straps and others by wing nuts or slot and stud. Tassets were roughly square in shape, and made from a sheet of solid metal, although shaped to give the impression of lamination. They were profusely decorated with dome-headed rivets.

Musketeers, who formed the other element of the infantry, did not wear any form of defensive armour.

Infantry officers, when they wore armour at all, favoured a more decorative version of the breast- and backplate, generally dispensing with the uncomfortably heavy tassets. When tassets were worn they were not the large squares of the pikeman, but a small variety shaped to the contours of the thighs and constructed of layers of metal riveted on the insides to leather straps, and providing freedom of movement. They were often works of great beauty with etched designs over the surface, and gilding to further enhance the effect. Much of this fine armour came from Milan and other cities of Northern Italy long famed as centres of the armourer's craft. For reasons of economy and weight most officers of foot contented themselves with wearing only a gorget for protection. This was a larger version of the pikeman's metal collar, worn without breast- and backplate. It came down to the breast-bone, being roughly triangular in front, and was usually decorated with etching or dome-headed rivets.

Dragoons

Dragoons, who were at this period mounted infantry, usually wore no armour, though some had a horse trooper's helmet, or a cabasset, which was a conical helmet with a shallow brim. Many dragoons wore a broad-brimmed hat—as did some of the cavalry—with a small steel skull cap called a secrete underneath. For dragoons taking part in the hazards of siege warfare a good deal more protection was required, and for this an extremely heavy version of the pikeman's armour was used, with a solidly made lobster-tailed pot—the tradi-

Above:
Top, a Dutch pot; below this is another single-bar zischagge, or lobster pot.

Below:
A pikeman's metal collar, hinged on the left; and an officer's more elaborate gorget.

Right:
Lobster pot, buff coat, bridle gauntlet and front- and back plates—demonstrating quite clearly, the 'proofmark' of the armour's resistance to shot.

tional cavalry helmet. On these occasions mobility was sacrificed for bulletproof security.

Cavalry Armour

A trooper of horse wore an eminently practical armour consisting of breast- and backplate over a buff coat, heavy leather top-boots, and usually a lobster-tail helmet. The left hand and arm, which held the reins, were often protected by a metal bridle gauntlet—a 'glove' with metal strips or laminations covering the back of the hand and the fingers. The glove was attached to a metal sleeve, into which the wearer's arm could slip above the elbow. The buff coat, of thick leather with long full skirts reaching almost to the knees, also gave protection from sword cuts, although it would not stop a bullet. Most buff coats had long sleeves and were fastened down the front by cross-lacing.

The best known helmet of the era was the zischagge, commonly called the lobster-tailed pot. The typical English version was a low-crowned affair, constructed in two halves, and joined along the comb. The neck guard or lobster tail, which gave the helmet its popular name, was constructed of a single piece of metal, shaped to give the appearance of overlapping strips. Triangular ear flaps, with leather chin thongs, were hinged at either side of the helmet. In front was a peak, loosely riveted at each side so it could slide up and down, with three metal bars fastened vertically providing protection from sword cuts to the face. Some versions of the helmet had a ridged peak with a single bar instead of three; this bar passed through a small hole in the peak, and being secured by a wingnut it could be raised or lowered as the occasion demanded. An imported type of this helmet with the single nasal bar, called a Dutch pot, had a ribbed skull and a small ring finial on top. Many lobster pots also had a small tubular-metal plume holder, so that the helmet could be embellished with ostrich feathers.

Cuirassiers

A few units of horse wore the full cuirassier armour. Those that did were nicknamed 'lobsters' and the best known among them was Sir Arthur Hesilrige's regiment. At the Battle of Roundway Down (1643) Hesilrige was shot at from close range with pistols, and slashed at with swords, but thanks to his armour he survived the encounter. His impregnability inspired Charles I—who was not a noted humourist—to reflect that 'had he been victualled as well as fortified, he might have endured a siege of seven years'.

Cuirassiers' armour was, in fact, three-quarter armour, as it ended at the knee. It comprised breast- and backplates, (with a laminated culet sometimes providing extra protection behind), and gorget similar to a pikeman's. A pair of large pauldrons (shoulder armour) were buckled to the gorget, and vambraces protected the arms. The upper cannon, from shoulder to elbow, was connected to the pauldrons by articulated strips of metal or laminations; the lower cannon was hinged to open, permitting the hand to pass through, and this was then fastened by a spring clip. The upper and lower cannons were connected to the elbow cop with loose rivets, so that the arm could bend freely. Stylishly shaped laminated gauntlets, with a central ridge ending in a pointed top, covered the hands. The thighs were guarded by shaped knee-length tassets composed of 16 or more small lames of metal, each overlapping to give an excellent articulated protection. The tassets terminated in a knee cop called a poleyn, whose fan shaped projection covered the back of the knee, and the poleyns buckled over the top of heavy riding boots.

Cuirassiers wore a variety of helmet. Many used the lobster-tailed pot, or an old-fashioned close helmet with either visor or barred faceguard. The close

Cuirassier's armour

Right: A contemporary break-down of cuirassier's armour. Below: A cuirassier's close helmet (top) and an open face close helmet of cuirassier pattern.

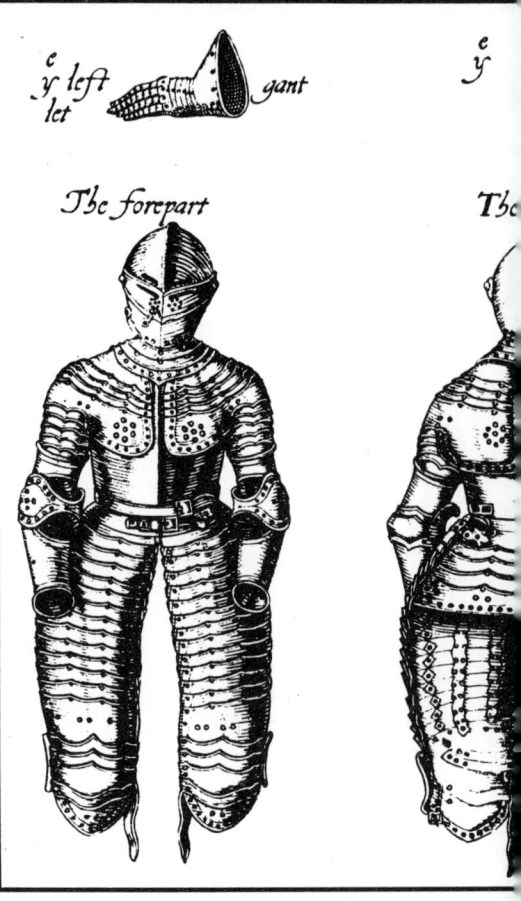

helmet generally had a low central comb to the skull which entirely enclosed the wearer's head and neck; the face was protected by an upper bevor with two horizontal slits or sights to see through. The upper bevor rested into the visor which was pierced with small holes called breathers; below the visor was the lower bevor, enclosing the wearer's chin. The bevors and visor were all pivoted from loose rivets at each side, and the parts of the helmets were held close by pivot hooks and staples.

A later version of this helmet, which was typical of the seventeenth century cuirassier, replaced the upper bevor and visor with a peak and vertically barred face guard. A variant of this was the savoyard from Northern Italy, whose plain face guard with eye holes and mouth slit resembled a sinister death's head.

Another popular helmet, worn either with cuirassier armour or simply a breast and back, was the burgonet. Unlike the close helmet, with bevors and visor riveted at the sides, it had hinged cheek pieces and a ridged visor. The burgonet's cheek pieces varied, some covering only the sides of the face and buckling under the chin, while others completely enclosed the face, closing with a pivot hook and staple. This variety had eye holes similar to the savoyard, and breath

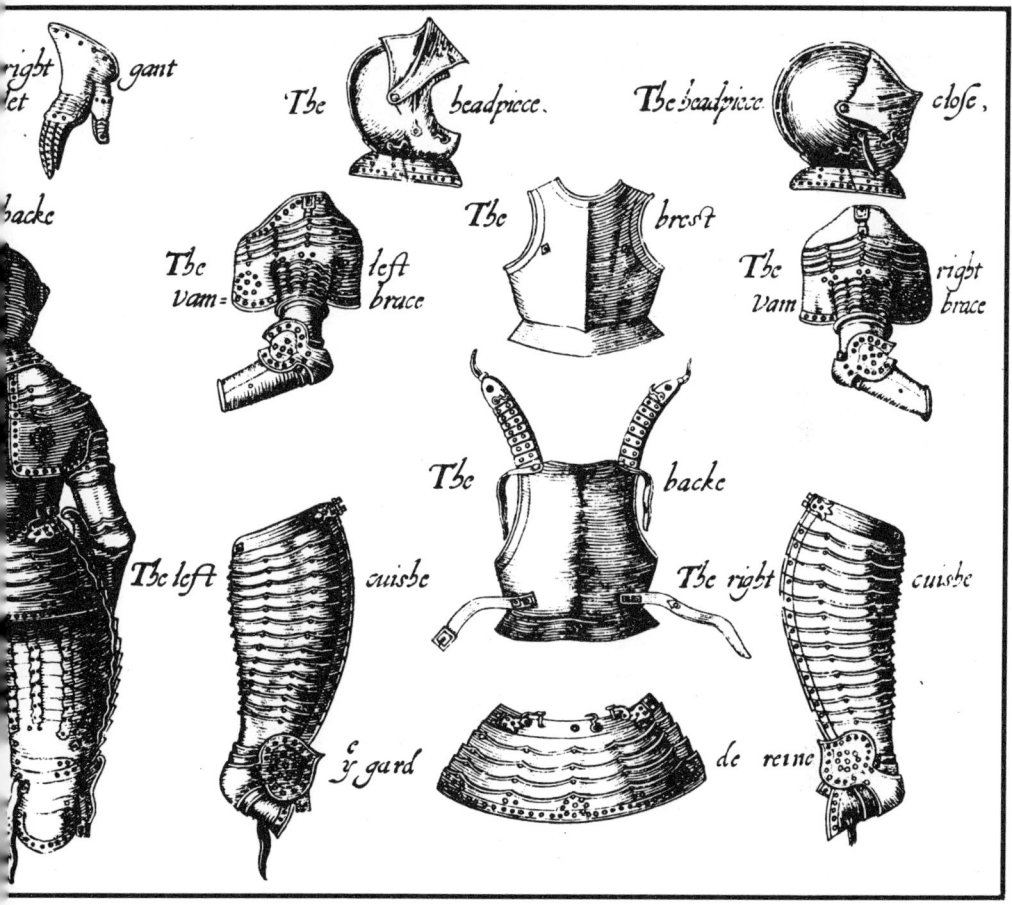

holes. Sometimes these helmets were simplified in the Civil War by the removal of much of the face protection and the addition of a nasal bar.

General Officers
Most generals, from the King downwards, had their portraits painted in armour of the cuirassier style, often embellished with fine etching and gilding. The appearance of the armour was still further enhanced by treating the metal surface with a blue or russet dye, which also helped to prevent rust. (The rank and file often painted their armour black, in the interests of preservation). But although senior officers were eager to be portrayed in full armour, in battle they usually found it preferable to compromise, and wore something that was more comfortable, if less safe.

Collections of Armour
All the most typical armour of the Civil War can be viewed at the Tower of London Armoury, and the Wallace Collection in London contains some particularly decorative examples. The finest collection of buff coats in England, and possibly in the whole world, is at Littlecote House, near Hungerford, Berkshire, together with a good general collection of weapons and armour belonging to the Parliament troops of Popham's Regiment.

by Richard Ratner

WEAPONS

The English Civil War came about during a period of transition in the history of weaponry; the seventeenth century witnessed both the decline of body armour—a protection which had been accepted for thousands of years—and the rise of the principal factor in that decline, the hand-held firearm, to a dominating position on the battlefield. Whilst firearms improved functionally and increased in numbers, so the profusion of edged weapons steadily declined; during the Thirty Years War the proportions of muskets to pike in the regiments had been gradually increasing, and the Civil War in England saw a continuation of this trend which was, by the end of the seventeenth century to witness the complete usurpation of the role of the pikeman by the musketeer, in the form of the bayonet.

Firearms lock mechanisms
The matchlock: During the Civil War several types of ignition were in use, the simplest, and certainly the most common being the matchlock. This had evolved from the firing mechanism of the early hand cannon, and simply involved the application of a lighted match to the touch-hole.

In the matchlock's favour was its cheapness and the ease with which it could be repaired, but its disadvantages were numerous. It required the musketeer to carry a lighted match, with the perpetual possibility (especially for poorly trained troops) of accidental discharge. On the other hand, if the match was not lit the gun could not be fired—a contributory factor in the Scots' defeat at Dunbar in 1650 was that one in four of their musketeers had been ordered to extinguish their matches, in order to avoid wastage. Indeed the sheer quantity of the match required by the matchlock was another of its shortcomings; during the siege of Devizes Hopton's Cornish infantry were so short of match that the town was ransacked for bedcords which might fulfill the purpose. Worse still, the matchlock was unreliable and the powder often took a long time to ignite. Finally, the weapon was cumbersome: it could not be used at all by horsemen, and the drill movements for loading and firing were many and tedious. Not surprisingly, alternative firing mechanisms were sought.

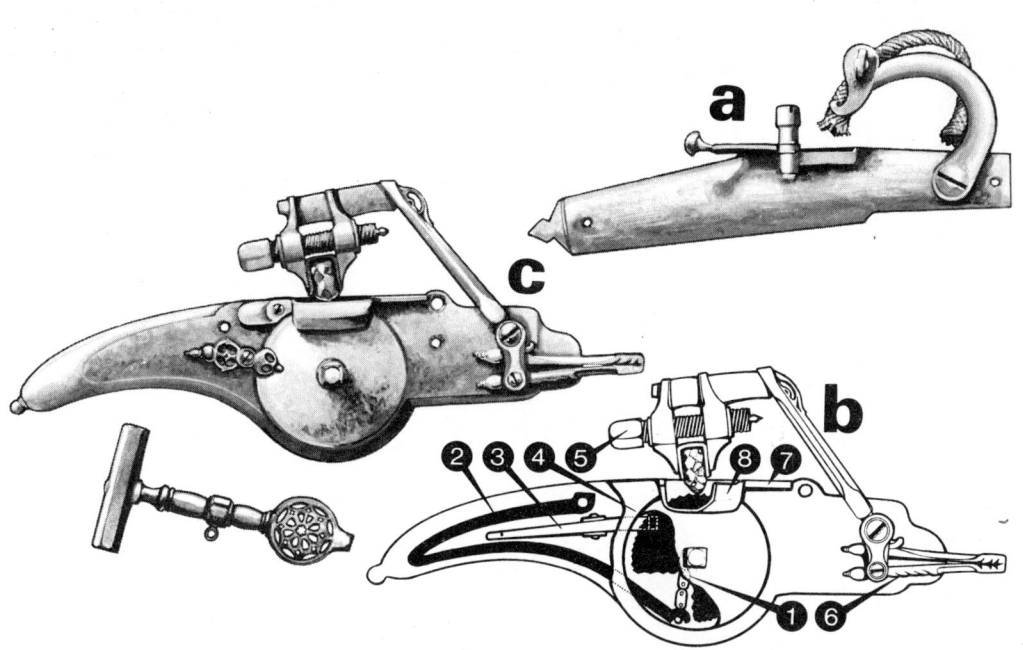

Above: a, matchlock; b, c, wheellock. Also shown is the spanner for winding up or 'spanning' the lock.

The wheellock: The origins of the wheellock are still uncertain, but it appears to have been invented in Germany or Italy at the very beginning of the sixteenth century. Its mechanism involved the combination of clockwork with a rotary friction surface.

To 'span' the lock one wound the spindle in the centre of the wheel with a spanner, thereby tightening the chain (1) attached to a powerful mainspring (2) which was compressed by the action. When the trigger was squeezed it pivoted a double sear (3) so that the sear-head (4) which protruded through the lockplate was disengaged from a socket in the wheel. This allowed the mainspring to expand, pulling the chain and forcing the wheel to revolve. The wheel had a serrated edge so that the dog (5), with a piece of iron pyrites in its jaws, having been pushed firmly into contact with the revolving wheel and secured in place in the pan (8) by the dog spring (6) gave off sparks which ignited the powder in the pan. The sliding pan cover (7) was automatically pushed open when the weapon was spanned.

The wheellock was certainly a far superior weapon to the matchlock, and could be fired from horseback; but it too had its disadvantages. It was a complex, relatively delicate mechanism, which was both expensive and took a long time to manufacture. The desirable compromise was a lock mechanism less complicated than the wheellock, but more efficient than the crude matchlock.

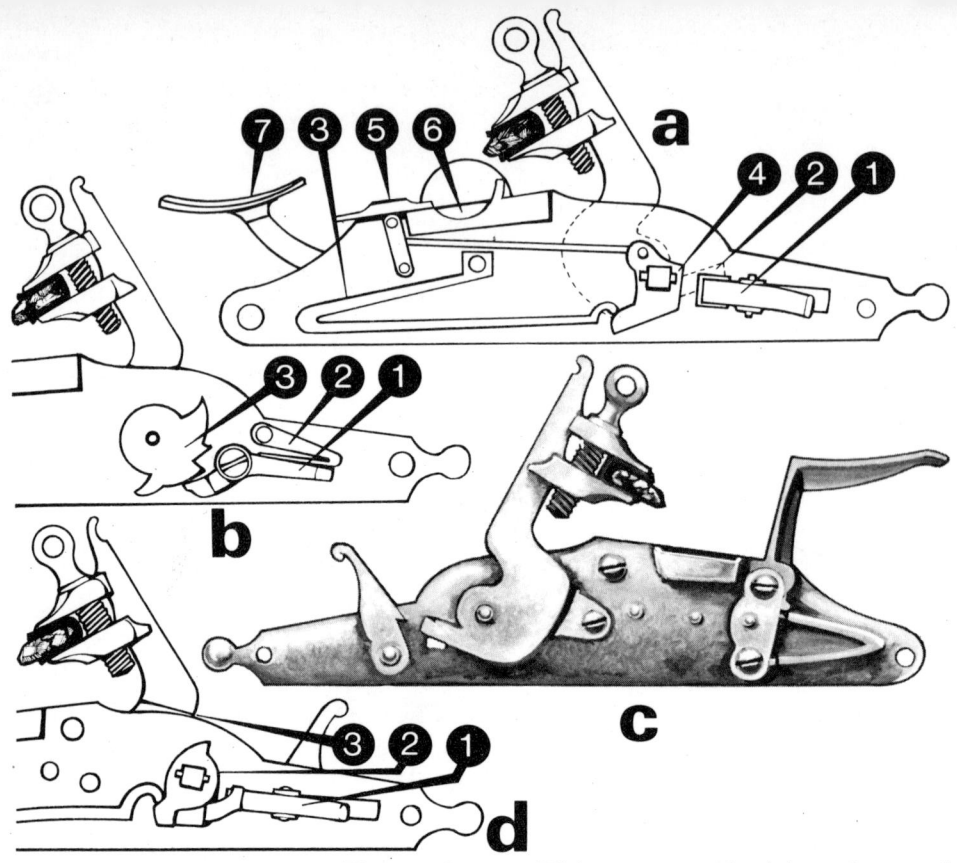

Above: a, snaphaunce; b, flintlock; c, d, English lock.

Opposite page: matchlock musket.

The snaphaunce: This appears to have been invented in Germany or the Netherlands about the third quarter of the sixteenth century, and was the prototype for a series of mechanisms culminating in the flintlock, which remained the standard lock mechanism in Europe until the second quarter of the nineteenth century.

When the trigger of the snaphaunce was pressed the sear (1) was disengaged from the heel of the lock (2). The mainspring (3) then forced the tumbler (4), which was attached to the lock, to revolve. The pan cover (5) was simultaneously forced forward, covering the pan (6). The cock, with a piece of flint in its jaws, then struck the battery (7) pushing it forwards and emitting a spark which fell into the pan, discharging the piece.

The flintlock: Around 1620 a modified snaphaunce appeared, which is termed the English lock, and by the time of the Civil War a variant of this had developed which more resembled the true flintlock than the snaphaunce — the dog lock. It still had a horizontally acting sear (1) but, instead of protruding through the lockplate, this now engaged the tumbler (2) in which

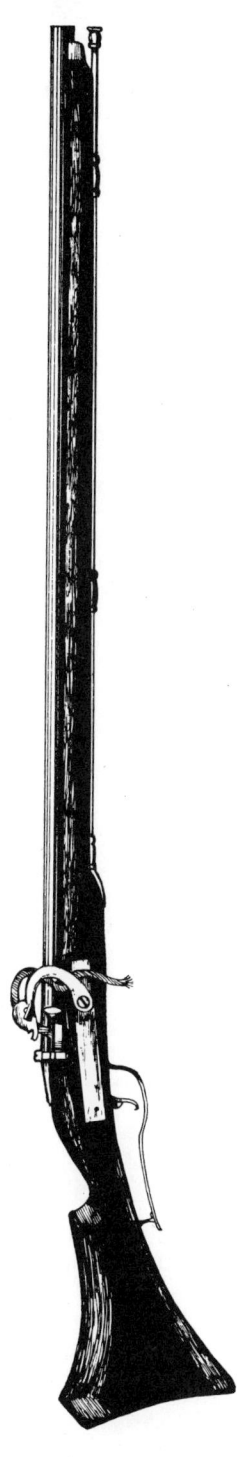

there were two notches—half cock for safety, and full cock. Additionally, a lip (3) was fitted to the inside of the cock, rendering obsolete the buffer used on earlier specimens to stop the cock from going too far forward.

The 'true' or French flintlock was also used in the Civil War although this was not common. The sear (1) was vertically active and held in place by the sear spring (2) engaging the tumbler (3).

Types of firearms
The shortage of weapons at the beginning of the Civil War made necessary the use of sporting guns and hastily repaired older weapons as well as newly manufactured military pieces; as far back as 1630 the Council of War had laid down specifications for the various types of firearms—but uniformity would have been less a reality than a pious aspiration.
The musket: This was the standard firearm of the infantry. With a barrel length of four feet and an overall length of about five feet, it was a large and cumbersome weapon. Firing a $1\frac{1}{4}$ ounce ball, it was nominally effective at a hundred yards, although its imperfections made it more suitable for volley firing than for careful aiming. The stock was usually of walnut and the butt was triangular (or 'fish-tailed') in form, following closely the Dutch pattern, and it was fitted with a matchlock. Because of its length and weight the musket required a rest, which was spiked at one end for fixing in the ground, and forked at the other to take the musket's weight.

As additional protection for the musketeers while they slowly reloaded their cumbersome pieces, the Swede's feather or swine feather, was introduced: this combined a spike with the musket rest, turning it into 'a half pike 7 or 8 foot in length, used after the manner of a rest . . . One of the them was enough to trouble a whole file'. The musketeers' logical defence, the bayonet, did not appear in England until well after the Civil War.

Other accessories for the musketeer were his bandolier—a belt on which hung about a dozen wooden cases each containing a musket charge, a bag for musket balls, and two wooden flasks—one for gunpowder and the other for the finer priming powder.
The caliver was a weapon of musket bore, but with its shorter barrel (39in) and lighter proportions it did not require a rest. It was fitted either with a matchlock or an English lock. Infantry regiments do not seem to have used it during the Civil War, although the 'firelocks' who guarded the Trains of

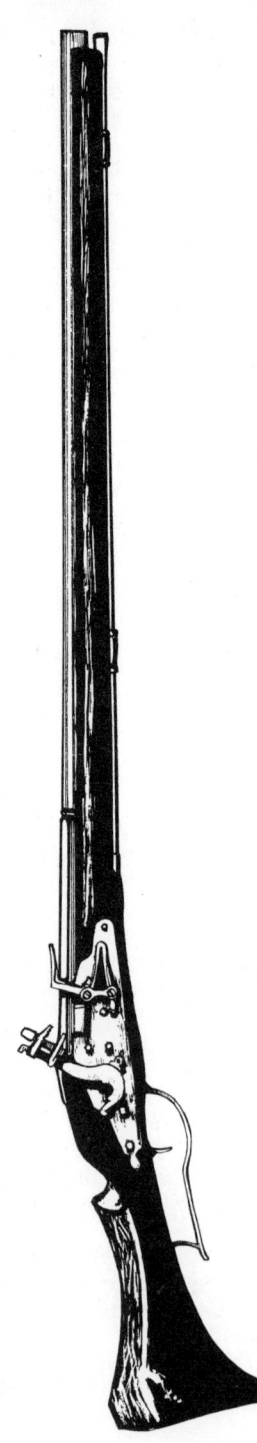

Artillery were equipped with calivers or fusils. It appears that the caliver in a matchlock or English lock form was the closest weapon to the dragoon musket. Dragoons were originally equipped with the dragon, described in 1625 as 'short pieces of 16 inches, the barrell and full musquet bore with fire locks or snaphaunces'. Very few dragons survive, so it is more than likely that the gun had been replaced by a dragoon musket, which was carried on a shoulder belt, and attached to it by means of a swivel.

The Carbine and Petronel: The petronel was a popular weapon among cavalry troopers in the last quarter of the sixteenth century. Its butt drooped almost at right-angles to the barrel (which according to the 1630 Regulations was to be 30in long) so that it could be held against the chest. (Its name probably is the anglicised form of the French dialect word 'petrinal' meaning 'of the breast or chest'.) However, by the time of the English Civil War the term petronel appears to have been used to describe a carbine. The carbine itself apparently ceased to be regulation issue when the New Model Army was formed, although officers may have carried it unofficially.

Left, musket and, above, pistol, both mounted with English locks.

Pistols: Primarily cavalry weapons, these were carried in holsters on the saddle bow. Three main varieties were in use during the Civil War: the wheellock, the English lock (which was fitted on contract pistols even when 'firelocks' were specified), and—just occasionally—breech-loading rifled turn-off pistols with a French flintlock. (These were loaded by unscrewing the barrel and inserting the charge and ball at the breach.) It must have been this last type of pistol that Prince Rupert is supposed to have used for his famous demonstration of marksmanship when he hit the weathervane of St. Mary's Church, Stafford, from a garden sixty paces from the foot of the tower.

Miscellaneous firearms: In addition to orthodox regulation military firearms both sides utilised any guns that they could obtain. Both fowling pieces and hunting rifles were employed to notable advantage. The rifled barrel gave additional range and accuracy and was particularly valuable in sieges. During the Siege of Lathom House marksmen armed with 'screwed guns and long fowling pieces' kept watch 'to the great annoyance of the enemy, especially of their commanders who were frequently killed in their trenches or as they came and went from them'. When Sir Lewis Dyve held Sherborne for the King two gamekeepers with fowling pieces picked off four Roundhead officers and gunners in their main battery. The value of these weapons was so appreciated by General Monk that in his *Observations* he proposed that six men in each company should be equipped with fowling pieces to act as sharpshooters.

Edged Weapons

At the outbreak of the war the Parliamentarians lacked only firearms, whereas the Royalists were also desperately short of edged weapons. Clarendon described how in the foot in the early years of the War, 'three or four hundred marched without any weapon but a cudgel' and 'in the whole body there was not one pikeman had a corslet, and very few who had swords'.

Swords: Two main categories of sword were used in the Civil War—the broadsword, for cut and thrust, and the rapier, which was purely for thrusting. The typical English broadsword of the period had a double-edged three-foot blade. Its basket-hilt, often crudely chiselled with a head, gave it the nickname 'mortuary sword', because it was thought that the head symbolised Charles I. This theory must be false, however, because most of the so-called mortuary swords can be dated earlier than 1649, the year of the King's execution.

Also fitted with a mortuary hilt was the backsword, which had only one cutting edge. Broadswords and backswords were carried by the foot and horse of both armies, but a smaller sword, called a hanger, was made for the foot. This weapon had a basket hilt or a knuckle-bow, and a broad, curved, single-edged blade about 26in in length. The shorter blade made this a more practical arm for foot soldiers than the rather clumsy broadsword.

The other major type of sword, the rapier, was fitted with a narrow, long, double-edged blade, designed for thrusting. The guard was usually of cup or dish form to protect the hand, and the hilt was fitted with a knuckle bow. It is quite common to find the mortuary head chiselled on the guard of rapiers of this period. The rapier, which contemporaries often called the tuck, was carried by the horse and by foot officers. Most of these weapons are of superior quality to the back- and broadswords.

The sword was normally carried on a belt slung over the shoulder, which was called a baldric, and

Below, 'mortuary' broadsword.

was made of leather or cloth and often richly embroidered. The sword fitted into this, or alternatively into a sword carrier of five straps, which was suspended from a baldric or a waist belt. This latter form, extremely popular in Elizabethan times, had been virtually discarded by the mid-seventeenth century.

The Pike: Was the standard arm of the foot. According to Monk it should have been 18ft in length, but later it appears to have been reduced to 16ft; an order of 1657 calls for 3,500 pikes 'to be made of good ash 16 feet long', at 3/4d each. Even then it was quite common for a soldier to reduce the length of his weapon to make it less unwieldy. The pike head was of steel, sometimes with a reinforced armour-piercing point, and was attached to the wooden shaft by metal side-straps about two feet long. These prevented the head being sheared off by cavalry swords.

The Halbert: By the time of the Civil War the halbert was more a badge of rank than an offensive weapon, though Sir John Byron's portrait shows him with an ugly halbert scar received in a skirmish at Burford. The halbert, for cutting or thrusting, was a spike with an axehead below it, mounted on a shaft and between 7ft and 8ft in overall length.

The Partisan: Like the halbert this was primarily a badge of rank carried by officers of foot. It had a broad flat blade, with projections on either side known as flukes.

The Spontoon: This was a partisan with leaf-shaped head and cross-piece, serving the same purpose as its relative. It was sometimes called a half-pike.

The Pole Axe: Though a weapon of the fifteenth and sixteenth centuries, the pole axe was still used by Civil War cavalry, especially on the Royalist side. A combination axe-head, hammer, and armour-piercing spike, it was a very effective weapon against heavily armoured horsemen upon whom the sword would have had little effect.

The Lance: Had been discarded in England by the time of the Civil War, but the Scots cavalry still used the 'staff' or light lance. At Marston Moor one squadron of Lord Balgoney's lancers 'charged a regiment of the enemies Foot and put them wholly to the rout'. In Ireland the Scottish lancers were so effective that Owen Roe O'Neill equipped one troop in each of his Irish cavalry regiments with the lance. But generally speaking the lance played only a small role in the Civil War, and did not reappear in English service until the formation of lancer regiments in 1816.

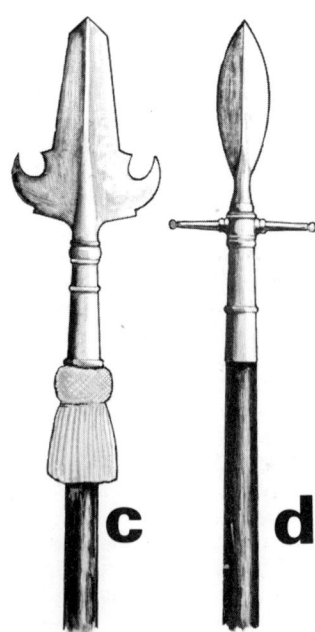

Above: a, pike; b, halbert; c, partisan; d, spontoon.

DRILL

by Edward Surén

'The first Rudiments of education, wherewithall to enter young Souldiers ... ought to be the well managing and handling of their Armes, which may easily be attained by frequent Practice, and the Souldiers thereby be brought to use them with ease, safety, and delight' (Barriffe, Military Discipline: or the Young Artillery-Man, *1635*)

Accustomed as one might be today to the snap and crackle of infantry drill, the drill as practised in the seventeenth century would appear to be cumbersome, not to say sloppy. It must, however, be remembered that the weapons were in fact almost as dangerous to the owner as to his enemy: therefore it was essential that drill—the 'postures'—be carried out with care and, if possible, grace. It should also be borne in mind that the average soldier would neither be much accustomed to mass discipline, nor of excessive intelligence (always excepting, of course, the gentlemen who wielded 'the more honourable Arms', especially on the Royalist side, and the more reliable veterans of the New Model Army in the later stages of the war.)

Elton (1668) defined the perfect private soldier as one who ought to 'avoid all quarrelling, Mutinies, Swearing, Cursing or Lying, and to be content with his wages, and likewise to be a good husband in the well managing of his means, keeping himself neat and handsome in his apparel; avoiding Drunkeness, and all manner of Gaming; truly to serve and fear God, and be obedient to all the commands of his superiors, cheerfully going upon all duties and to be loving, kind and courteous unto all his fellow Soldiers'. Such a paragon must have been rare indeed; all the more reason that drill be carried out slowly, carefully and with elegance.

The contemporary drill illustrations on the following five pages are reproduced from The Military Discipline wherein is Martially showne the order for Driling the Musket and Pike set forth in postures with ye words of comand, and brief instructions for the right use of the same (Sold by Tho. Jenner at the foote of the Exchange in London 1642); *and* Military Instructions for the Cavallerie *by John Cruso, 1644.*

Musket drill

Since the musket of this period was generally a matchlock, it was essential that a most meticulous drill should be observed. The match was held between the first and second and the third and fourth fingers of the left hand whilst priming and loading; at the order 'cock your match' it would be fastened into the 'serpent' ready for firing. It was important to blow off any loose powder around the pan after priming in order to prevent a premature discharge—which in a fairly dense mass of men could be very dangerous.

Reserves of powder were held in a budge barrel to the rear of the musketeer formation, and the charges carried by each man were refilled therefrom. Again, it was advisable not to dip into it with the left hand, as the resulting explosion would be fatal to many. This type of accident did in fact frequently occur among badly trained musketeers.

'Have a care' (the 'order arms' position, and the basic starting point for musket drill as well as for pike).

'Draw forth your scouring stick' (in order to ram home the bullet and charge).

The 'poize' position, the essential linking posture between the 'have a care', 'shoulder your musket' and 'present upon your rest'.

'Blow off your loose powder'.

'Present upon your rest', or the 'sentinel posture' (when the musket is charged, primed and cocked).

'Give fire'.

49

Pike drill

The pike being a weapon of inordinate length—sometimes as long as 16ft or more, the pikemen were chosen from the strongest and tallest men in the unit. It was generally considered to be rather fashionable to 'trail the puissant pike'.

Pike drill was basically more simple than musket drill and depended for its effectiveness on numbers, to produce the 'hedgehog' front to charging horse, and to provide a tightly-knit mass of pike and armour for 'push of pike'. When on the march, the pike would normally be shouldered, but according to Elton's *The Compleat Body of the Art Military* the pike might also be shouldered in the immediate presence of the enemy: 'For it much preserveth the Pikes and Pikemen, from the danger of the shot, the bullets then gliding off from their Arms; which if they stood at such times, either ordered, or advanced; the bullets would make such a chattering amongst the Pikes, that what with breaking of them, and the shivers flying from them, may much endanger the Soldiers which shall carry them.'

'Have a care', or 'order arms'.

'Port your pike'

Cavalry drill

A troop of horse drawn up for service would have been led by their Captain, followed by two trumpeters half a horse's length behind him to right and to left, and his cornet. The front rank would have been flanked by the 1st corporal on the right, the 2nd on the left, while the 3rd and 4th corporals would have been similarly posted in the rear rank. The lieutenant would have brought up the rear.

With the obsolescence of the caracole, the principal arm of the cavalry became, once again, the sword; however, the cavalry were armed with pistols, and sometimes with carbines as well. The pistol was carried in a holster on the saddle whilst the carbine hung from a sling on the right-hand side of the rider: to all intents and purposes, the drill for each was similar to musket drill, although carried out on a somewhat less stable platform than for the foot.

A harquebusier on the march.

'Spann your Pistoll' (The main cavalry firearm would have been the wheellock pistol.)

'Present and give Fire'.

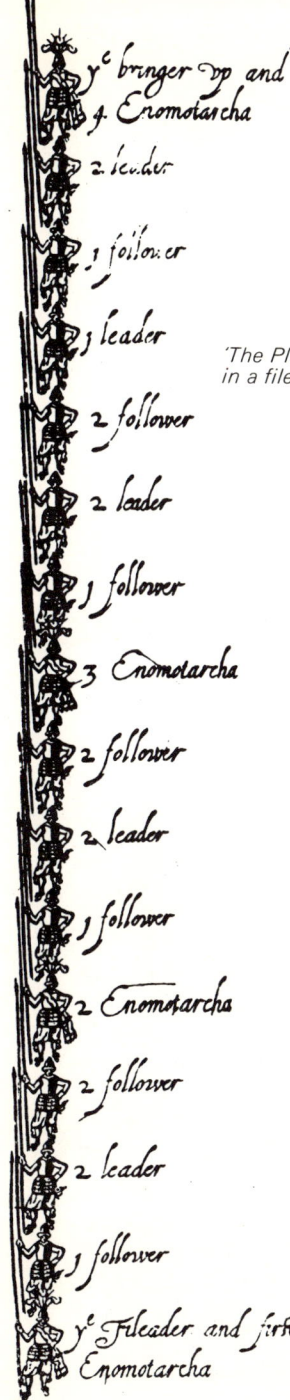

'The Places of Dignity' in a file of pikemen.

THE NEW MODEL ARMY

Foot: Twelve Regiments, each with 1200 men in 10 Companies. The Colonel's company had 200 men, the Lieutenant-Colonel's 160 and the Major's 140 with the other seven having 100 men in each. These were commanded by a Colonel, Lieutenant-Colonel and Major as field officers with three officers to each company—Captain, Lieutenant and Ensign. The Colonel's company was usually commanded by a Captain-Lieutenant as with Horse. There were two drummers to a company and the New Model Army had a ratio of two musketeers for every pikeman in the regiments.

Horse: Eleven Regiments, each with 600 men plus Officers, in 6 troops of 100 men. These were commanded by a Colonel and Major as field officers and four officers to each troop—Captain, Lieutenant, Cornet and Quartermaster. NCO's in the troop were 3 corporals. Normally the Colonel's troop was commanded by the Senior Lieutenant as Captain-Lieutenant. There were three trumpeters to a troop.

Dragoons: One Regiment of 1000 men divided into 10 Companies of 100 men. Commissioned officers were as in the Horse and NCO's as in Foot regiments. There were two drummers to a company.
   Additionally regiments had staff officers attached for provost, clerical, spiritual and medical duties.

Artillery: A strong train of artillery was given to the New Model Army. Whilst the details are lost, C. H. Firth quotes Fairfax's train in 1647 as containing 16 demi-culverins, 10 sakers, 15 drakes and 15 smaller field pieces—in all 56 guns, besides mortars and battering cannon for siege use. Light field pieces were usually attached to infantry regiments.
   The train and baggage of the army in 1647 required 1038 horses and were guarded by 2 companies of firelocks.

Artillery

'. . . a spunge that can never be filled or satisfied.' (Clarendon)

by Peter Morton

By the beginning of the seventeenth century artillery was a science tempered with art, which, because of its associations with the 'black arts' was steeped in its own mystique. The much quoted Monluc who said 'Il fait plus de peur, que du mal,' ('it frightens more than it hurts'), was stating a fact which in certain circumstances still holds good in the twentieth century, if the ratio of casualty figures to rounds fired is analysed. The master gunner of the period understood the effect, if not the cause, of most factors influencing the behaviour of projectiles. 'Heavy air' was known to affect trajectory even though the work of Torricelli was not widely published.

A Culverin and a Cannon mounted upon platforms in the manner which would have been employed when firing from prepared positions during a siege. This also illustrates the use of the quadrant for ascertaining the elevation of the piece necessary to achieve the required range.

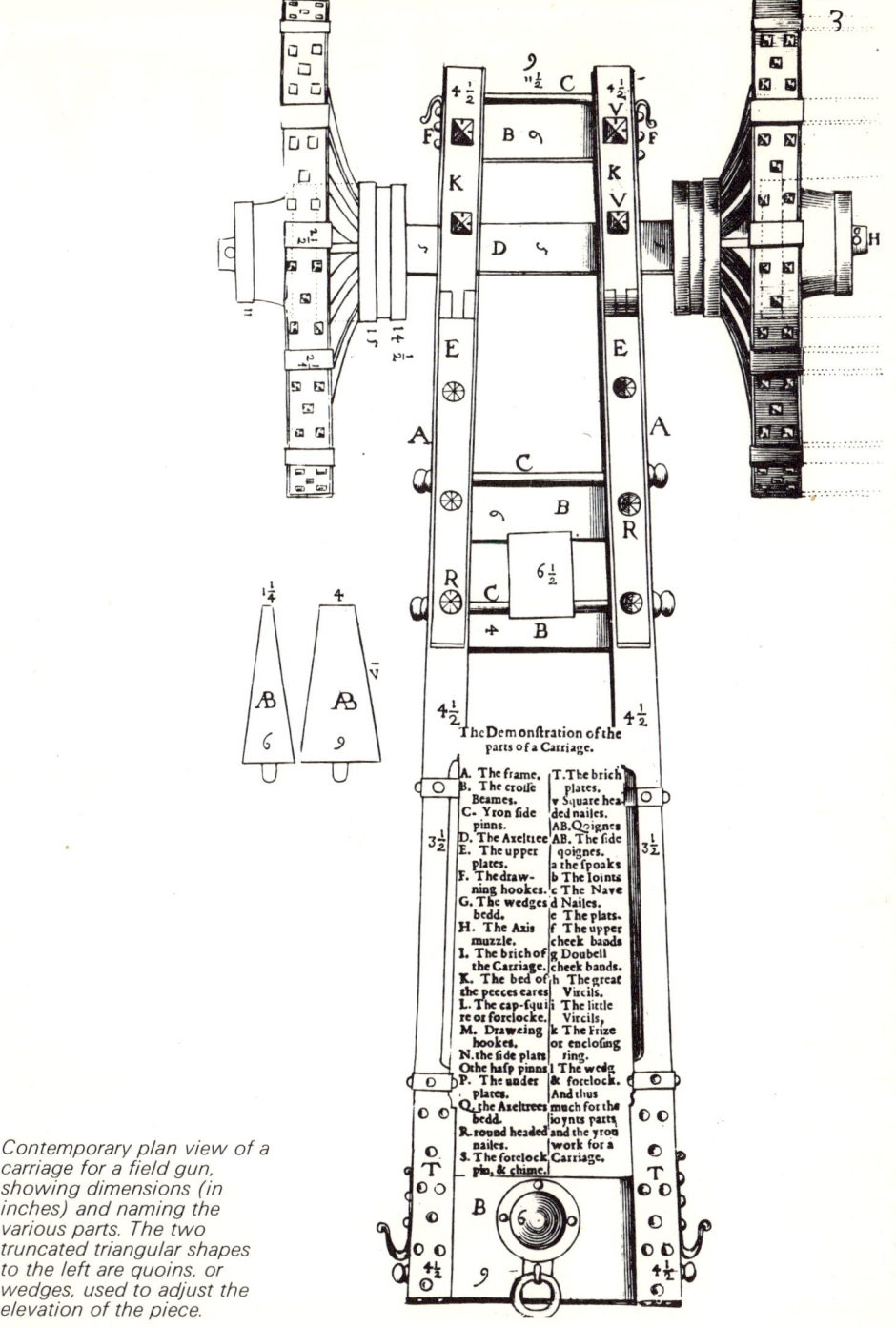

Contemporary plan view of a carriage for a field gun, showing dimensions (in inches) and naming the various parts. The two truncated triangular shapes to the left are quoins, or wedges, used to adjust the elevation of the piece.

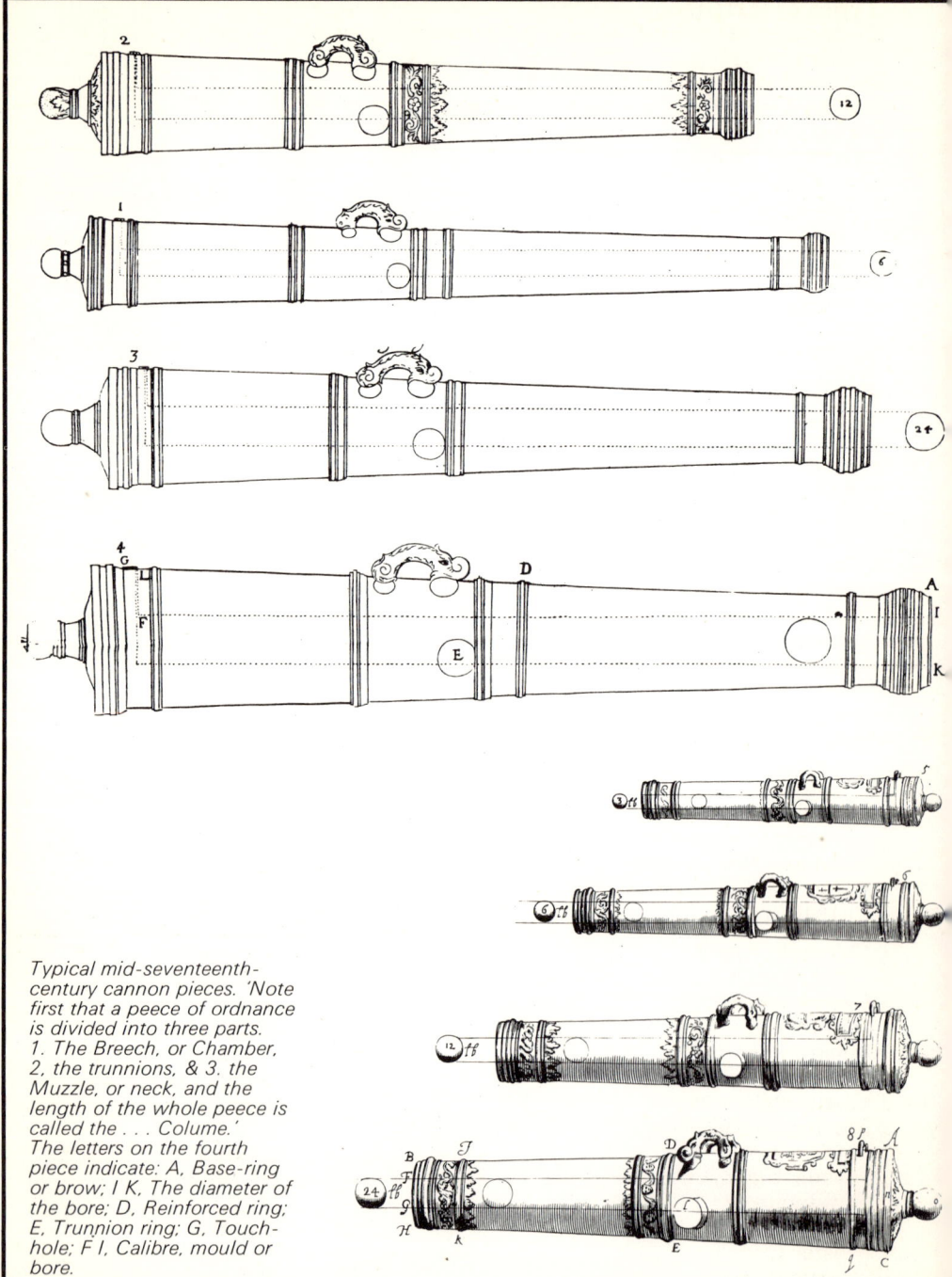

Typical mid-seventeenth-century cannon pieces. 'Note first that a peece of ordnance is divided into three parts. 1. The Breech, or Chamber, 2. the trunnions, & 3. the Muzzle, or neck, and the length of the whole peece is called the . . . Colume.'
The letters on the fourth piece indicate: A, Base-ring or brow; I K, The diameter of the bore; D, Reinforced ring; E, Trunnion ring; G, Touch-hole; F I, Calibre, mould or bore.

Types of Artillery

To appreciate the make up and problems of a typical artillery train one must first examine the properties and performance of the guns, bearing in mind that standard nomenclature and bore dimensions were not established until much later.

	Weight of Shot	Calibre	Weight of Charge	Weight of Piece	Number of Men to Draw	Number of Horses to Draw	Point Blank Range	Maximum Range
CANNON ROYAL	63lbs	8in	40lbs	71·5cwts	90	16	300yds	1500yds
CANNON	47lbs	7in	34lbs	62cwts	70	12	360yds	1740yds
DEMI-CANNON	27lbs	6in	25lbs	53.5cwts	60	10	340yds	1600yds
CULVERIN	15lbs	5in	18lbs	41cwts	50	8	400yds	2000yds
DEMI-CULVERIN	9lbs	4.5in	9lbs	22.3cwts	36	7	380yds	1800yds
SAKER and DRAKE	5lbs	3.5in	5lbs	14.3cwts	24	5	300yds	1500yds
MINION	3.7lbs	3in	3.5lbs	10.5cwts	20	4	280yds	1400yds
FALCON	2.5lbs	2.7in	2.5lbs	6.2cwts	16	2	260yds	1200yds

It would seem from these figures that the optimum piece to give good range, projectile weight and mobility was the culverin of 15lbs. Such a gun in good condition would be capable of firing 8 rounds an hour, or 10, given time to cool every few hours. Using a weight of corned powder approximately equal to the ball weight, together with wadding and match it will readily be seen that to support such a gun during an eight-hour battle would need one ton of materials, and all such stores would need transporting in carts drawn by oxen or horse teams. In addition to the guns and ammunition, carts, tentage, spare harness, mobile forges and coopers' carts there would be the principal officers' personal effects, the whole making a ponderous accompaniment to an army travelling the indifferent roads of the day. It was small wonder that an army without a train was known as a 'flying army'.

The establishment of a typical train, that of James I in 1618, was:

1 General of Artillery	1 Petardier
1 Lieutenant-General	2 Waggon makers
1 Comptroller	2 Gabion makers
1 Commissary	2 Harness makers
10 Gentlemen of the Ordnance	1 Cooper
25 Conductors	2 Farriers
2 Comptrollers of Fortification	1 Surgeon
1 Master Gunner	1 Surgeon's mate
136 Gunners	1 Captain of Miners
1 Master Fireworker	25 Miners
2 Conductors of Fireworkers	1 Captain of Pioneers
2 Battery Masters	25 Pioneers
1 Master Carpenter	1 Trench Master
12 Carpenters	1 Waggon Master

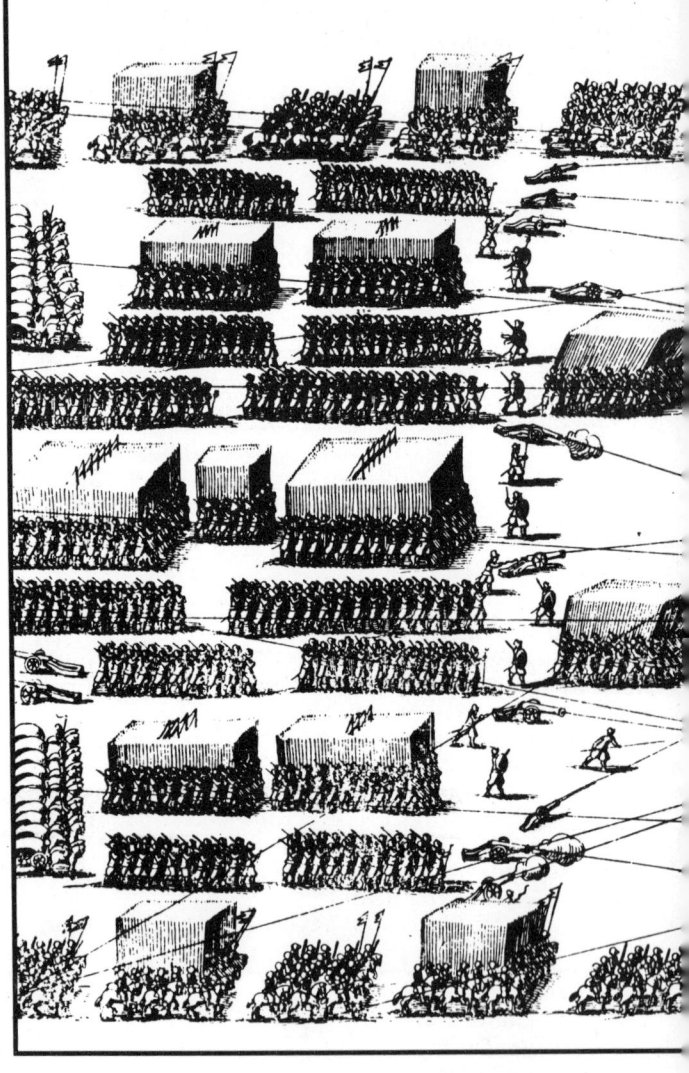

A 1642 opinion of how artillery should be placed on the field of battle by a commander, 'whereby he maye annoy most an Ennemy'.

These personnel would be supplemented when the need arose by the intake of matrosses and waggoners, the latter being civilians employed on a casual basis. The pay of this train was about £20 per day in the currency of the period during peace time. Certainly this expense would not have been borne unless the military value justified it.

The conduct of the train in the field depended greatly on the relationship between the General of Artillery and the Commander-in-Chief of the army. A General of Artillery who could rely on support

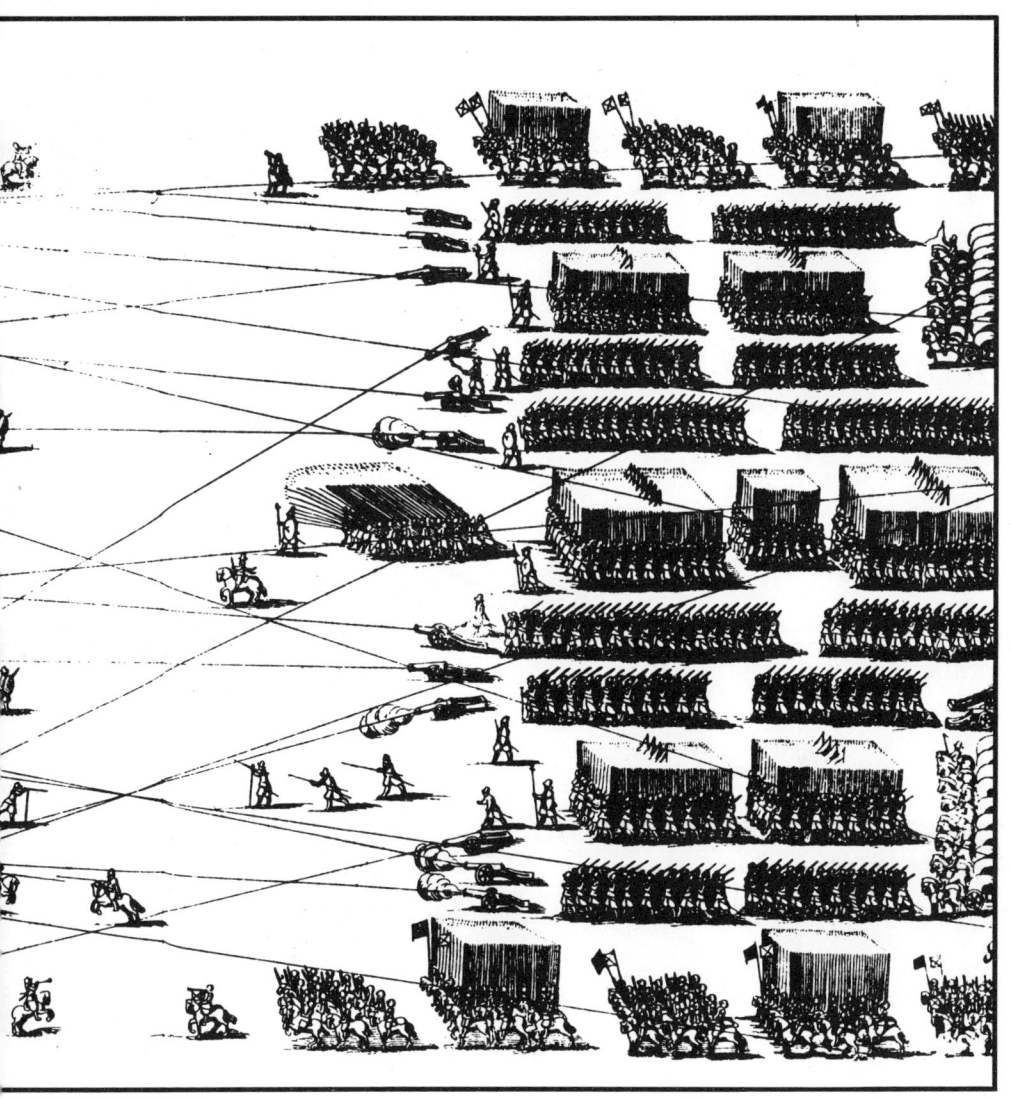

from the horse and foot could afford to fight a more open battle than one who needed to group his guns for mutual protection. When the co-ordination between units was of a high order, the lighter guns could be placed in groups, forward on the field, between bodies of foot. The guns would, where possible, be protected by defences of wickerwork, basket-like gabions filled with earth, and would rely on their own cavalry to protect them from the oblique charges of enemy horse who would attempt to overrun the guns. The effectiveness of the guns

The transport of artillery according to Hexham (1642): Top frame shows how to haul artillery when horses are unavailable. The numbers of men required to pull various sizes of artillery were all carefully calculated: 'For a quarter canon, carriage, attelage and all, will weigh 3000 pound weight, now allowing to every man 60 pound weight to drawe, everyone of these 8 pieces require 43 men: so that for these 8 quarter canons you must have in all 344 men, which being ... divided into three equall files and distances, each drawing rope must have 14 men and one odd man over, to goe by.' Second frame shows a half-canon mounted on its carriage 'drawne with seven couple of horse and a Thiller horse'. 'But if the way be foule, morish, and durty, then for a whole canon, weighing 7000 lb. weight, you must spanne in 15 couple of horse and a Thiller ...' Similarly, for a 'half-cannon' one would need 11 couple and a thiller; for a 'quarter cannon' 6 couple and a thiller; for a Falconet 2 couple and a thiller; and for a 250 lb. Drake just one horse. 'You must observe' continues Hexham, 'also that the mettle of one of the States half canons weigheth ... 4500 pound weight, the carriage of yron work there-unto belonging about 900 pound, so that these [15] horses are to drawe in all the weight of 5400 pound, and the other peeces proportionately.' The third frame shows the use of wheelbarrows for moving munitions over short distances, whilst the bottom two frames show the versatility of the 'Block or Long waggon' for carriage either of pieces or other things, such as punts or pontoons—'boats to clapp a bridge on a sudden over a river'.

depended on the skill of the principal gunners in cutting the correct fuze lengths, choosing the correct missile and angle of fire for each situation, and laying the guns. Typical engagements began with an artillery exchange when the opposing armies were 800 to 1,500 yards apart. Solid spherical shot of stone, lead, or iron, was used with moderate charges, which on hard ground would cause the missiles to bounce several times before coming to rest. When the enemy began to move forward shell was used from 800 yards range down to 300 yards, the object being to achieve air-bursts whose fragmentation effect might break the charge before it gained momentum. At 300 yards cannon were used in the manner of shotguns, discharging langridge or 'hail shot', containers of iron pieces or musket ball; the last round was usually double loaded, the possibility of a burst barrel at this stage taking second place to the need to prevent the guns being overrun and 'nailed'.

Gun Drill

The words of command given for firing a 'peece' by William Eldred, with explanations:
1. *Put back your peece*. Necessary because of the recoil of the previous shot.
2. *Order your peece to load*. Remove the elevating wedge and depress the breach in order to elevate the muzzle to assist loading.
3. *Search your peece*. A staff with a spike at right angles to its length was introduced into the breech and to remove smouldering debris from the previous shot.
4. *Sponge your peece*. Wet and dry mops were used to suppress smouldering residue and soften hard-cake fouling.
5. *Fill your ladle*. The powder ladle was taken to the budge barrel of gun powder and filled with powder. The ladle was designed to hold the measured charge for a particular type of gun and was made in such a way that it would empty its contents into the breech when rotated through 180°.
6. *Put in your powder*. The ladle was thrust down to the gun breach.
7. *Empty your ladle*. The ladle was rotated and withdrawn.
8. *Put home your powder*. A rammer was thrust into the bore to lightly compress the charge in the breach. At this stage the gunner in charge placed his thumb on the vent to prevent powder being forced out.
9. *Thrust home your wad*. Wadding was placed in

the bore and rammed down onto the powder charge to form a piston against which the propellant gases would push.

10. *Regard your shot.* The gunner would examine the projectile, checking if necessary with a gauge to make sure it was of the correct diameter. 'Windage' or clearance in the bore was generally $\frac{1}{4}$in. Should the shot show cavities or irregularities the gunner would attempt to load the ball with such imperfections in line with the axis of the bore in an attempt at stabilisation.

11. *Put home your shot gently.* The projectile was seated onto the wadding with the rammer; should too much force be used the granules of 'corned' powder would be crushed and inconsistent results obtained.

12. *Thrust home your last wad with three strokes.* This was the overshot wad which prevented the ball moving away from the driving wad.

13. *Gauge your peece.* By giving directions to his crew the gunner laid the gun on target, using the elevating wedge under the breach end of the barrel and swinging the trail end of the carriage to the left or right.

The gun was now ready to fire. The gunner rammed a priming iron through the touch-hole or vent to make sure it was clear. He then either placed a fuse in the vent or topped it to overflowing with fine mealed powder. The piece was touched off with a gunner's staff, a linstock holding a piece of smouldering cotton rope. The staff was necessary to keep the gunner clear of the recoil of the carriage.

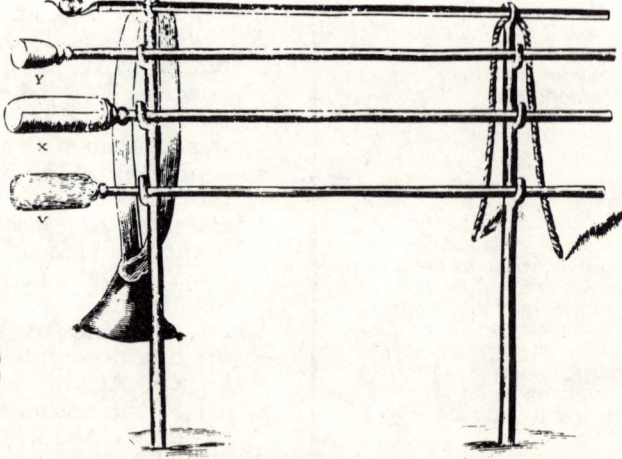

Some of the tools used for serving the guns as illustrated in Malthus' Pratique de la Guerre *(1631). At the top is a wad hook; below this is the rammer, powder scoop, and the sponge. Also shown (not to the same scale) are a pair of calipers, used to ascertain that the shot would fit the bore of the piece.*

Below:
Making 'Granadoes, both great and small, to be shot, or cast out of a Morter, and also ... Hand-Granadoes, to be cast into a Trench, a Sapp, or the worke of an Enemy'. One recipe for making bombs recommends 3 parts of cannon powder 'well pounded and sifted', $\frac{1}{3}$ part of 'Greekish pitch, & halfe the weight thereof in brimstone'. These were to be mixed, supplemented by $\frac{1}{2}$ part of ordinary salt and kneaded 'well together, with oyle of linseed'. This mixture would have filled the hollow shell, and through a touch-hole sealed with coarse linen smeared with pitch and wax, would have protruded the fuze, 'an artificiall match'.

Siege Artillery

It was at sieges that artillery played its most effective role. The attacking army having cut off the garrison from outside help, the gunners laid down 'dismounting fire' with their lighter field pieces to drive the defenders from the walls, whilst the heavy siege pieces were brought up. Planked wooden platforms guarded by gabions and earthworks were constructed by the engineers and pioneers to receive these guns, which then concentrated their fire on the weakest part of the defences in order to breach them and give access to the foot soldiers. Mortars or pot pieces would be used when available, exploiting their high trajectory to throw bombs and incendiary materials over the walls onto the more vulnerable buildings beyond. At times, sewage and carcasses were projected in this manner to add to the discomfort of the defenders. In places where the country surrounding the besieged works was unsuitable for ground-laid gun platforms, raised earthworks called 'cavaliers' were constructed for this purpose. It was necessary to have a firm flat surface along which the guns could move without interruption in order that the recoil energy could be harmlessly dissipated as motion which, if prematurely checked, would cause the rapid disintegration of the carriage. This problem was not overcome until the advent of spring and hydraulic recoil damping systems.

Lighting the fuze (A) on a bomb (or 'Granado') prior to firing a mortar during a siege (note the gabions in front of the mortar). The ignition is carried out by means of a portfire (B). Note also that the bombs (C) appear to be conveniently provided with handles, for ease of loading.

SIEGE WARFARE

by Christopher Duffy

While it is easy to be attracted by the dash and excitement of the field actions in the Great Civil War it should not be forgotten that many a district of Civil War England can also tell of a more protracted and obstinate struggle—a war of trenches, ramparts, palisades, bombardments and blockades.

It was a matter of elementary prudence for the rival parties to secure their respective capitals—Royalist Oxford and Parliamentarian London—by large and strong works of fortification. The course of the war very soon showed that the other defensible positions were hardly less important, for a solid rampart and a powerful garrison could confirm the allegiance of productive citizens, protect trade and communications, and guarantee snug quarters for an army during the winter months. A town was trebly valuable if it stood by a harbour or navigable river: it was hardly less vital for the Royalists to hold on at Chester, for instance, than for the Parliamentarians to retain London.

Some of the fortified towns were situated in such a way as to offer a considerable 'nuisance value' to the other side. For years on end the Parliamentarians of the north-east Midlands were plagued by the Royalists who had ensconced themselves so impudently on the middle Trent at Newark. Conversely the Parliamentarians had a centre of resistance at Gloucester which disrupted the communications between the Royalists of Cornwall, Wales and the Oxford region. More pernicious still was the influence of the Parliamentarian garrisons of Plymouth, Lyme and Taunton, which effectively paralysed the south-western Royalists during the fatal Naseby campaign of 1645.

The countryside between the towns was fought over by the garrisons of smaller posts. Around Oxford the Royalists had troops in Banbury,

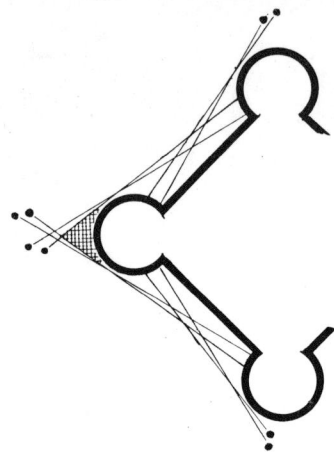

Woodstock, Boarstall House, Brill, Wallingford, Faringdon and Abingdon, as well as garrisons in the distant southern outposts of Donnington Castle and Basing House. For a comparable 'strategic region' on the other side we may cite the Gloucester Parliamentarians who had fixed themselves in Tewkesbury, Sudeley, Newnham, Beverstone and Slimbridge, as well as in the *centrum mali* at Gloucester itself. Small garrisons such as these had a radius of activity of at least ten miles, within which they led an exciting but not unduly dangerous life, preying on couriers and military and commercial traffic, organising parish contributions, and collecting information about enemy designs. If needs be they could assist friendly armies by taking charge of their sick and their surplus artillery.

Fortification

On the Continent the art of military engineering had made considerable progress since the time when the tall masonry walls of the mediaeval castles were able to bid defiance to enemy catapults for months or years on end. Everything was changed by the coming of mobile siege guns in the 1490's. The architects of the Italian Renaissance were the first people to build fortresses which could withstand the new artillery: they made the walls thicker and lower-lying than in earlier days, and they trimmed the old towers into four-sided angular works called 'bastions', which could mount a good deal of artillery, and which were so designed as to eliminate any 'dead ground' by which the besieger might have approached the foot of the wall unscathed.

In their Eighty Years War (1566–1648) against the Spanish the Dutch took over the Italian bastioned ground-plan, but built their fortifications of earth, instead of masonry. An earthen rampart was cheap and easy to build; it offered almost unlimited resistance against artillery fire, and when suitably planted with palisades it was just as difficult to climb as a masonry wall.

Both the Royalists and the Parliamentarians were eager to employ foreign experts who had direct experience of these modern Continental methods — people like Rupert's right-hand man Bernard de Gomme, who was a Walloon, or the hard-drinking Dutchman John Dalbier, who helped to capture Basing House for Parliament in 1645, but then changed sides and died a hero's death at St. Neots in 1648. Furthermore there were hundreds of native Englishmen who had served in the Dutch, Swedish, Spanish or Imperial armies, and who returned to their homeland with a pretty fair idea of how

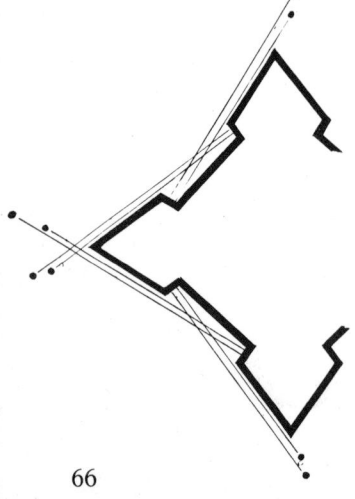

Mediaeval and 'bastioned' ground plans, showing how the bastion trace eliminated the 'dead ground' which had been present at the salients of the mediaeval towers. Above is the ground plan of part of a typical mediaeval fortress: the towers are round, and consequently there is an area (shaded) in front of each tower which cannot be searched by the fire from the neighbouring towers. In contrast the plan below shows the bastioned layout, where the towers have been reshaped into angular bastions with outward-facing 'faces' and sideways facing 'flanks'; each part lies in careful geometrical relationship with the others, and the patch of 'dead ground' has now been eliminated.

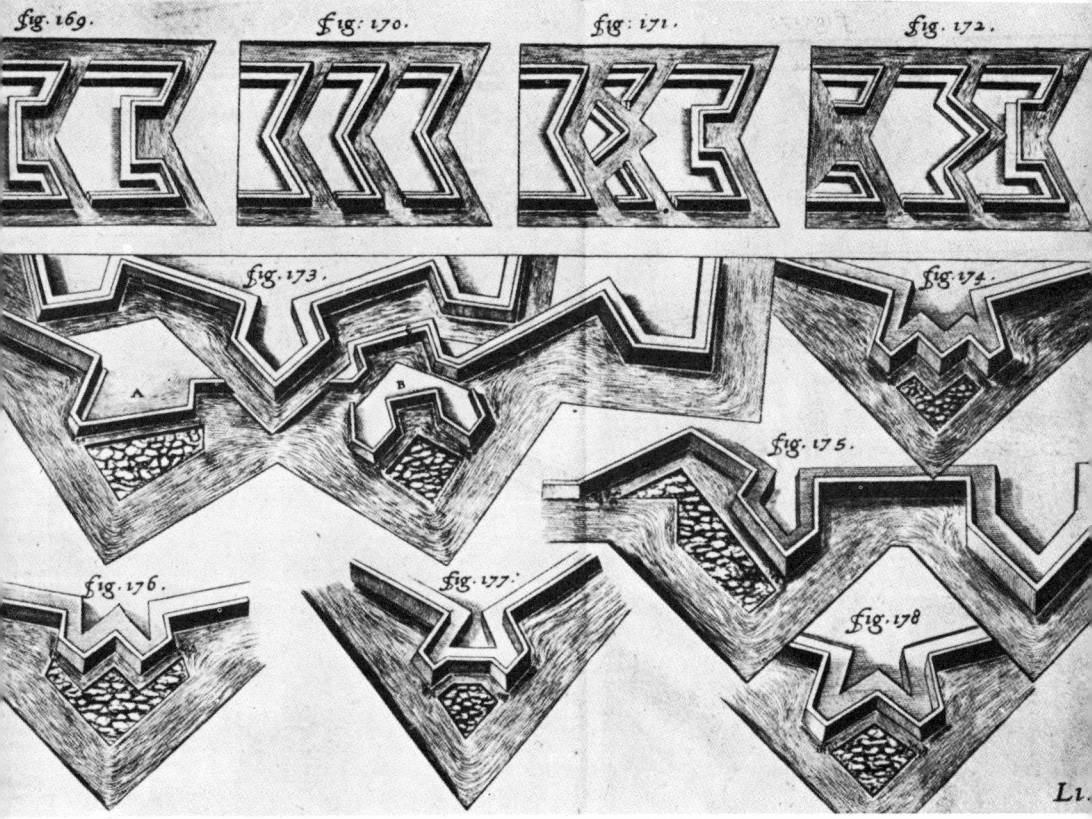

fortifications were built and how sieges were carried on.

What was lacking was not so much technical expertise as the time and resources to apply engineering plans on such an ambitious scale as on the Continent. Very occasionally (as at Oxford and Newark) we encounter passable imitations of Continental town 'enceintes', with bastions and curtains. However at London, Chester, Plymouth and Bristol the engineers decided that it was more economical to surround the towns with a perimeter made of a breastwork and ditch, which was reinforced every few hundred yards by a bastioned fort or redoubt (a redoubt being a small square or triangular work which was enclosed on all sides, and not open to the rear like a bastion). Cheaper still was the practice followed at Worcester and King's Lynn, where earthen bastions were simply added to the old town walls. Free-standing bastions were liberally scattered around towns of all sorts in order to cover dead ground or hold the enemy at a distance: there

Retrenchings—the typical seventeenth-century system of covering defended positions by other fortifications, and isolating sections lost to the enemy. The basic idea was that, though the attackers might take a bulwark or hornwork, they would have gained but little, still having to face further lines of fortification. 'Figs 169–172' show methods of cutting off 'crowne-workes' and 'horne-workes', while 'Fig 173' shows the retrenchment of a wall or rampart. 'Figs 174–8' demonstrate the cutting off of bulwarks.

are 'sconces' of this kind at Reading, Worcester, Newark, York and Newcastle.

Manor houses and castles were reinforced in styles which were far too numerous to enumerate here, though it is worth mentioning that Basing, the most famous of the fortified houses, was strengthened in the Civil War by a new perimeter of earthen bastions. Often, however, the old strongholds were left to face the enemy with little or no modern protection. At places like Bodiam, Chepstow and Ludlow we may still see how dangerously close the venerable walls lay to the Parliamentarian battery positions.

Siegecraft

Most of the veterans of the foreign wars had at the back of their minds the knowledge of how the great Continental soldiers like Spinola or Frederick Henry of Nassau set about a formal siege. The first thing the army did was to dig itself into a fortified position of its own, from where it could beat off sorties from the fortress or interventions from the rear by an enemy army of relief. The breastwork and ditch facing the country was called the 'line of circumvallation', and the similar position confronting the fortress was termed the 'line of countervallation'.

The siege proper began when the engineers directed the soldiers to throw up one or more redoubts in front of the 'line of countervallation' and within a few hundred yards of the fortress. From these redoubts the besiegers drove a number of winding trenches towards the fortress, taking care that the arms of the zig-zags were safely defiladed from the fire of the towers and ramparts. Wickerwork baskets called 'gabions' were arranged along the side of the trench facing the fortress, and the earth from the excavation was shovelled inside so as to form a continuous parapet. The closer these trenches or 'saps' came to the fortress, the more bitterly was their progress contested. The head of each trench was protected from fire by a 'saproller', a large and firmly-filled gabion which was laid horizontally on the ground and pushed forward by the leading sapper. This brave (and short-lived) man was also responsible for planting the ordinary gabions and making the first cut of the trench; he was followed along by supporting sappers who dug the trench deeper and wider, and filled the gabions with the spoil. Still further to the rear, the soldiers threw up small redoubts at intervals along the trenches, so as to offer short-range support against sorties.

All this time the gunners would be maintaining a

fig. 156.

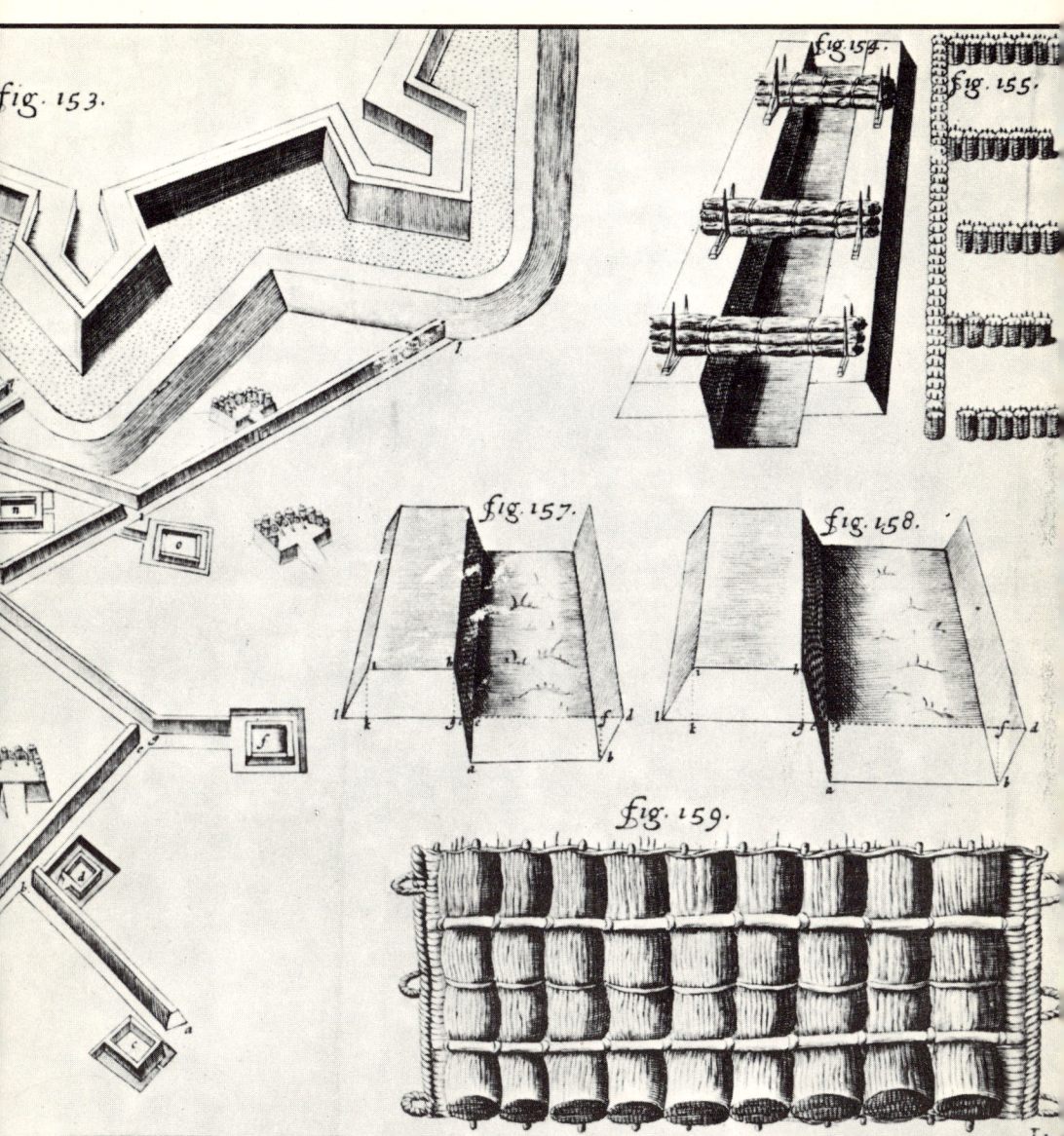

Siege warfare—the role of the engineer: 'Fig 153', a panoramic view showing the approaches to a fortified place, with parallels, redoubts and counterbatteries in place; 'Fig 154', where the ground was too hard to dig deeply, and enfilading fire could not be avoided, the method used was to make a bank of earth on each side and to place 'blindes' (bundles of brush or oaken planks) across the trench to give some measure of protection; 'Fig 155', where digging was impossible, gabions filled with earth and stones would have been used instead; 'Fig 156', this illustrates a different solution to the problem, merely consisting of redoubts built one before the other towards the enemy; 'Figs 157, 158', illustrate general profiles for trenches (though not parallels, which would have contained a firing parapet); 'Fig 159', is a section of a bridge of bullrushes, useful for crossing moats.

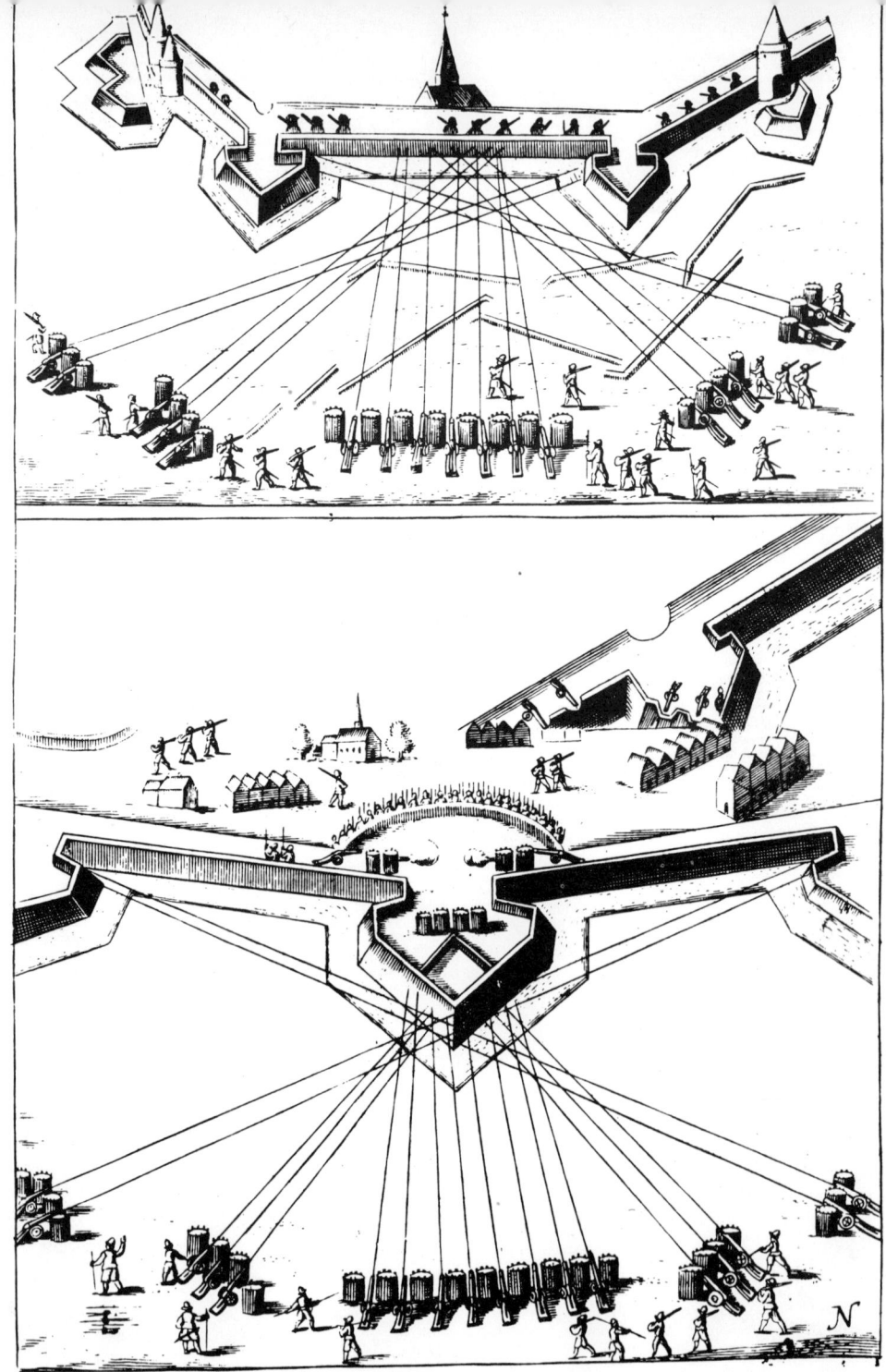

Left:
The use of artillery in siege warfare. The accompanying text to this illustration of 1639 discusses the relative merits of attacking a curtain or a bulwark, and throws light upon the effectiveness of properly planned and constructed defences. A bulwark might allow more elbow-room to the attacker, and give less resistance than a curtain, which would be defended by the crossfire from its neighbouring bulwarks; however, a bulwark could be isolated—shown crudely in the lower frame—so that the attacker would have yet another set of defences to contend with.

Below:
Seventeenth-century plan view of a 'trench-Cavalier', consisting of raised earthworks behind which are six wooden platforms for guns. The platforms themselves would be raised at the rear to counteract the recoil of the guns.

heavy fire to cover the march of the trenches. The most common siege cannon of the time were the 15–18-pounder 'culverins' and the 24–30-pounder 'demi-cannon', which threw a solid iron shot up to an effective range of about 600 yards. These guns were grouped in general-purpose batteries at any distance from 200 to 500 yards from the defences, and proceeded to dismount the garrison cannon, clear the rampart walks of troops, smash the palisades and wreck any masonry within range. The efforts of the cannon were seconded by mortars which lobbed explosive shells (cast-iron spheres filled with powder and ignited by a slow-burning fuze, weighing anything between 5 and 500lbs) at high trajectory.

The engineers, meanwhile, brought the trenches to the edge of the ditch. If the ditch were dry and the palisades and wall effectively breached, the crack troops of the besiegers would assemble in the heads of the trenches, then storm across the small tract of open ground and into the fortress.

Sometimes the way would be obstructed by an intact stretch of wall; in this event the siege miners would have to burrow into or under the masonry, and blow it into the air by a heavy charge of powder. A wet ditch would tax the ingenuity of the experts still further, for they had to pile up a causeway or launch a floating bridge so as to open a path to the breach.

The custom of the time considered that the lives of the defenders were forfeit, if they went so far as to compel the besiegers to deliver a storm. Not surprisingly most of the governors chose to capitulate on terms rather than bring affairs to this extremity.

The full glory of the mid seventeenth-century formal siege shines only fitfully in the English Civil War, and it is rare to find a place which, like Sherborne Castle in 1645, was subjected to something like the full repertoire of Continental siege techniques. Siege artillery was scarce, and so were trained engineering supervisors, but armies of relief were much more enterprising and quicker on their feet than similar forces on the Continent. All of this

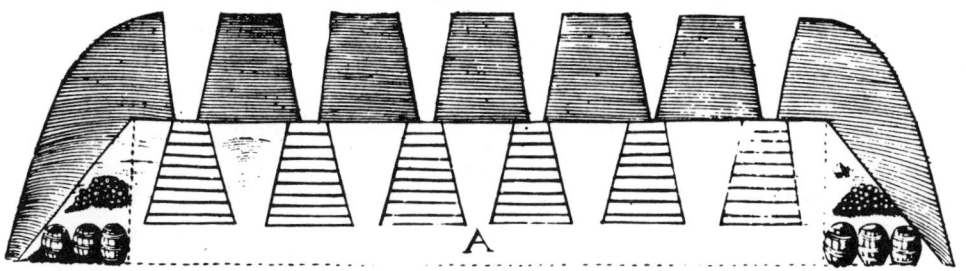

The petard was a well-tried method of blowing open the gates of a besieged town. It consisted of a metal pot containing explosive, fixed onto a board (known as a 'madrier') which in turn would be firmly fastened to the offending gate. The explosive force would be concentrated upon the gate, which should, if well fired, burst asunder. The petardiers would never have been as fortunate as the figures in this engraving, in having unimpeded access to the gates of a besieged fortress: indeed the actual placing of a petard must have been a feat of considerable skill and courage. Hexham (1640) recalls an incident during his service in the Dutch wars when 'having burst open one gate of the town the Petardier, hanging his pettard upon a second gate, a woman throwing a great stone down from the top of the wall feld the pettardier while he was doing his businesse,' and very effectively frustrated the attempt.

forced the English commanders to cut many corners in their sieges. Impatient people like Rupert, Fairfax and Cromwell were liable to throw in a mass assault long before their Continental counterparts would have considered that the state of the siege was ripe. Another time-saving expedient was to shower mortar bombs or red-hot shot into the town, so as to demoralise the defenders and citizens by the fire and destruction, as was attempted by Prince Maurice at Lyme in March 1644, and by the Parliamentarians at Chester in the autumn of the same year.

The countless smaller sieges were conducted in a spirit of 'do it yourself'. One characteristically English siege weapon was the 'sow', best described as a wooden tank which was propelled by the soldiers who crewed, or rather garrisoned, the vehicle. The sides were loopholed for musketry, and the men's feet could be seen dangling from the innards of the beast, rather like the trotters of sucking pigs, thus accounting for the name. In Nottinghamshire they specialised in a local variation called the 'testudo', which mounted a small mortar at the rear. In August 1645 Basing House witnessed one of the earliest essays in chemical warfare, when John Dalbier set fire to heaps of straw, sulphur and arsenic in an attempt to asphyxiate the garrison by the noxious fumes. This ingenious experiment, however, proved a total failure.

The rich variety of English fortress warfare in the 1640s has left much tangible evidence which survives to the present day. Almost every English county has shattered walls and bullet-holed doors which are capable of stirring the imagination more immediately than some empty battlefield. A townsman or countryman who has an interest in his locality can make a real contribution to historical research by observing, recording, and above all helping to preserve these relics of our past.

The Role of the NAVY

by *John Tucker*

The role of the navy in the English Civil War is often underestimated, the dazzle of Prince Rupert's dashing charges and the achievements of Cromwell's Ironsides tending to obscure the vital, if less spectacular, war that was waged by sea.

The fact that the bulk of the fleet fought on the Parliament side was of immense importance to the final defeat of the Royalist forces. Parliament's coup in seizing control of the fleet made possible the easy transport of men, stores, and equipment to succour

Model of the Naseby, *an 80gun Third Rate built in 1655 at Woolwich. Less austere than most Commonwealth vessels she was renamed* Royal Charles *after the Restoration. The figurehead of Cromwell on horseback was burned in 1663, and its replacement by a costly figure of Neptune was noted by Pepys. (National Maritime Museum.)*

the ports and cities held by Parliament garrisons—and these in turn supplied the essential logistic back-up to the armies in the field. So it was that Parliament's setbacks were never decisive: Waller, after defeat at Lansdown was able to recuperate in Bristol (then in Parliament's hands) in time to be beaten yet again at Roundway Down eight days later; and after Essex's disastrous campaign against the King in the summer of 1644, the navy was at hand to save the Lord-General from being taken.

Transport by sea was also faster than by land—the state of seventeenth century roads providing adequate explanation for the slow rate at which armies marched. Parliament's naval resources were more than sufficient compensation for the King's 'internal lines of communication', waging war from Oxford.

Just as important as this transport facility by sea was the denial of the same to the Royalists: communications with the Continent were effectively cut by the Parliament blockade, preventing Charles from more actively pursuing offers of help from his royal neighbours. Throughout the war, the King never gave up hope that help would come—if not from abroad, then from nearer at hand —from Ireland and Scotland. In spite of Montrose's brilliant campaigns, however, Scottish help came to the Royalist cause too late and when the Presbyterian faction had already made its contribution to Parliament's victory. Irish troops did land, meanwhile, though never in sufficient force to sway the course of events. The Parliament navy's vigilance prevented more than a slow and irregular influx via Chester and Bristol, and Charles' hope of help from Ormonde remained an illusion.

Seventeenth-century warfare on land was, by its very nature, indecisive. The capitulation of fortified towns and cities was generally followed by a gentlemanly exchange of the honours of war, and the freedom of the defeated garrison, sometimes (depending upon the negotiating talents of the governor of the town) even to the extent of retaining their arms (conduct difficult to understand for twentieth-century time-dwellers, after three-quarters of a century of total war). But half-heartedness was prevalent on both sides throughout the war, more dangerously on the Parliament side, and this in itself worked against an early decision. In spite of seemingly crushing victories on the field of battle, it took time to bring the war to a conclusion: it was the navy which ensured for Parliament the staying power to outlast the Royalist effort, and to win the war.

The mid-seventeenth century navy

With the death of Elizabeth I in 1603, the Navy had begun to run down. This happened so quickly that by 1617, the fleet had dropped to less than 30 ships of war—many of them unfit for sea. Pirates and privateers on the other hand went on increasing their activity in English waters and it was not until the end of James I's reign that steps were taken to overhaul the fleet. Even then the building programme was for no more than two ships a year, and the only vessel of consequence to be laid down was the *Royal Prince* of 90 guns, launched in 1610. Lavishly carved and gilded, she was a forerunner of the style of ship decoration typical of the second half of the century and the first departure from the boldly painted Elizabethan vessels. After the failure of the expeditions to Cadiz and La Rochelle in 1625 under the impulsive Duke of Buckingham, relations deteriorated with Spain and France. In the Navy, morale and capability were low; Turkish pirates raided the English coast and the Dutch fished inside territorial waters with the utmost contempt for the protests of Charles I.

It was against this background that the Ship Money Tax was levied in order to raise a fleet. Two writs were issued in 1635 and the third in 1636 led indirectly to the Civil War through the stand of John Hampden.

All too little is known of the Navy in this period. A list made for the Lord High Admiral in 1640 gives details of masts, sails and rigging. Names of vessels also exist, but other than a few sketches and some paintings by the Van de Veldes dating from the end of the 1640s, information is sparse.

The *Sovereign of the Seas* is an exception. Launched at Woolwich in 1637 and carrying 100 guns, she displaced about 1,500 tons—400 tons more than any other ship afloat. She was the first three-decker in the Navy and survived a distinguished fighting career through the Dutch wars when she was known as the 'Golden Devil'. The *Royal Sovereign* (as she later known) cost £40,000 (the equivalent cost of five or six Second Rate ships) and her splendid exterior was in lavish contrast to the miserable conditions for her crew within. Both the *Sovereign of the Seas* and the *Royal Prince* launched 25 years earlier were the work of Phineas Pett, a shipwright of remarkable genius.

Throughout the reign of Charles I, the long, low Elizabethan prow remained, although as new ships were launched the beakhead became shorter and more up-swept. The ships of the time were built without the earlier sternwalk but the side galleries remained, becoming more ornamented—as did the gun ports with their encircling gilt wreaths. The overall appearance of the Civil War navy, therefore, was broadly similar to that of the Elizabethan period, although by the beginning of the war the bonaventure mizzen or fourth mast had disappeared and the ships set a square mizzen topsail and a spritsail topsail. Gradually through the period the superstructure fore and aft became lower and the hull form broader at the waterline to cope with the heavier ordnance. The Royal ships would have been gay and colourful whilst the fleet of the Parliament was painted a 'sad colour'.

The principal guns with which they were armed in the Civil War were:
Demi-cannon   (32pdr) range 340yds
Cannon-Perier (24pdr) range 320yds
Culverin   (18pdr) range 400yds
Demi-Culverin (9pdr) range 400yds
Saker   (5pdr) range 340yds

The guns were mounted in broadsides on the upper and lower decks. A 40gun Second Rate (the backbone of the fleet) might have carried an armament comprising 4 Demi-Cannons, 4 Cannon-Periers and 32 Culverins, demi-Culverins and Sakers. Third and Fourth Rates carried Culverins, Demi-Culverins and Sakers. The rate of fire was slow with 10–12 shots an hour for the heavy guns and rather more for the light ones. It was not until the latter part of the century that the practice of mixed gun batteries ceased and cannon were rated by their weight (e.g., 32pdr).

The need to rank ships by size and capacity began in James I's reign, and during the war and the Commonwealth this reached a stage when Rates were first accepted. Even then they were only a general guide as they changed with the evolution of ships and methods of fighting. Batten's survey of the fleet in 1642 includes only three First Rates (one of but 40 guns). These would have been 100ft or more in length with a beam of about a third of this. Second Rates were up to 100ft, Third Rates up to 96ft, Fourth Rates up to 90ft, and both Fifth and Sixth Rates up to 60ft.

The Parliament Fleet
Two fleets went to sea each year—the Summer Guard from May to October and the Winter Guard from November until April. Both were supplemented by the hire of armed merchantmen, substantially built, readily available and useful in shallower waters.

In 1642, the list of ships in the Summer Guard commanded by the

1642 Fleet Survey by William Batten

First Rates	date	tons	men	guns	fit for (years)	
Sovereign	1637	1,522	600	90	15	
Prince	1641	1,187	500	70	20	
Merhonour	1616	946	350	40	5	
Second Rates						
Defiance	1616	857	250	38	2	(Summers only)
Rainbow	1617	731	240	40	10	
Constant Reformation	1619	742	250	40	7	
Victory	1620	721	260	40	7	
Swiftsure	1621	746	260	46	5	
St. Andrew	1622	783	260	42	10	
St. George	1622	792	260	44	10	
Triumph	1623	776	300	44	7	
Vanguard	1631	751	250	40	5	
Henrietta Maria	1633	793	250	42	9	
Charles	1633	810	250	44	9	
Unicorn	1634	767	250	46	9	
James	1634	875	250	48	10	
Third Rates						(Perhaps
Assurance	1601	600	200	34		2 Summers)
Dreadnought	1613	552	140	30	3	
Convertine	1616	621	200	34	3	
Antelope	1619	512	160	38	7	
Happy Entrance	1619	539	160	30	7	
Garland (sometimes spelt "Guardland")	1620	567	170	34	8	
Bonaventure	1621	557	170	32	8	
Swallow	1634	478	150	34	10	
Leopard	1635	516	160	34	10	
Lion	1640	620	170	40	20	
Fourth Rates						
Mary Rose	1623	321	100	25	4	
Expedition	1637	301	110	14	5	
Providence	1637	304	110	14	5	
Fifth Rates						(Perhaps
Eighth Whelp	1628	162	60	14		2 Summers)
Tenth Whelp	1628	186	60	14		
Sixth Rates						(4 years
Henrietta Maria (pinnace)	1624	68	25	6		Harbour Service)
Greyhound	1636	128	50	12	7	
Roebuck	1636	90	45	10	—	
Nicodemus	1636	105	50	6		(Perhaps 2 Summers)

Earl of Warwick as Admiral in the *James* (48) and William Batten as Vice Admiral flying his flag in the *Rainbow* (40) shows 24 merchant ships in service. Their tonnage ranged from 50 tons to 700 tons and ten of them were 400 tons or over so that in size the larger vessels would rank broadly with Third Rates.

The Royalist Fleet

Whilst the Parliament achieved control of the Navy and dominance of the sea, it must not be assumed that the Royalists were inactive. As the first Civil War progressed, they built up a major fleet of small ships used for privateering and the carrying of stores, ammunition or despatches. They

The highly ornate stern of The Sovereign of the Sèas, *100 guns, launched in 1637. She was built by Peter Pett (shown in this picture by Lely) from the design of his father Phineas Pett. (National Maritime Museum.)*

maintained links with Europe and ferried troops from Ireland. In the Spring of 1644, the Earl of Warwick reported to the House of Commons that the Royalists had 250 ships ranging from 50 to 600 tons and he needed 50 ships and 5000 men. The result was the authorisation of an expanded Summer Guard and the deployment of more small vessels to hunt down the privateers.

The rejuvenated fleet

The Navy which learned its discipline in battle and on blockade during the war regained also its self-confidence. It developed rapidly during the Commonwealth and Protectorate with Cromwell seeing the need for new ships and the vital importance of sea power. In 1654 more than 20 warships were launched and over 200 joined the fleet during the Interregnum. With Prince Rupert at sea it was necessary to protect the coast, England's increasing world trade and also to balance the rise in influence of the Dutch. Under Blake, the English fleet guarded the Channel, the Irish and North Seas, with units stationed in the West Indies and the Mediterranean. England became a sea power in a manner quite different from that of the brilliant gentlemen adventurers of Elizabeth's reign.

bibliography

by Lewis S. Winstock

This bibliography is selective, and many obscure works on the War have been omitted. So too have articles in periodicals and learned journals. The bibliography is essentially military and does not include books which have, primarily, a political, constitutional, economic, or social bias. All the listed titles should — hopefully — be obtainable through lending libraries.

The dates after each work refer to the edition which is likely to be most readily accessible to the general reader, and not necessarily to the date of original publication.

General
Burne, A. H. and Young P.: The Great Civil War, 1642–1646 (1959)
Clarendon Earl of: The History of the Great Rebellion (1888)
Firth, C. H.: Cromwell's Army (1967)
Gardiner, S. R.: History of the Great Civil War 1642–1649 (1903)
Lindsay, J.: Civil War in England (1954)
Wedgwood, C. V.: The King's War 1641–1647 (1957)

Battles and Battlefields
Morris, R. H.: The Siege of Chester 1643–1646 (1924)
Toynbee, M. and Young, P.: Cropredy Bridge 1644 (1970)
Wenham, P.: The Great and Close Siege of York 1644 (1970)
Woolrych, A. H.: Battles of the English Civil War (1961)
Young, P.: Edgehill 1642 (1967)
Young, P.: Marston Moor 1644 (1970)

Regional Histories
Abel, H.: Kent in the Great Civil War (1901)
Bayley, A. R.: The Great Civil War in Dorset (1910)
Broxap, E.: The Great Civil War in Lancashire (1910)
Bund, J. W. W.: The Civil War in Worcestershire (1905)
Coate, M.: Cornwall in the Great Civil War and Interregnum 1642–1660 (1930)
Clode, C. M.: London during the Great Rebellion (1892)
Dore, R. N.: The Civil War in Cheshire (Cheshire Community Council Vol. 8)
Farrow, W. J.: The Great Civil War in Shropshire (1926)
Godwin, G. N.: The Civil War in Hampshire (1905)
Guttery, D. R.: The Great Civil War in Midland Parishes (1951)
Johnson, D. A. and Vaisey, D. G.: Staffordshire and the Great Rebellion (1964)
Kingston, A.: Hertfordshire in the Great Civil War (1894)
Kingston, A.: East Anglia in the Great Civil War (1894)
Leach, A. L.: The History of the Civil War in Pembrokeshire and on its Borders (1938)
Ketton-Cremer, R. W.: Norfolk in the Civil War (1969)
Reckitt, B. N.: Charles I and Hull 1639–1645 (1952)
Thomas-Stanford, C.: Sussex in the Great Civil War and Interregnum (1909)
Tucker, N.: North Wales in the Civil War (1958)
Varley, F. J.: Cambridge during the Civil War 1642–1646 (1935)
Varley, F. J.: The Siege of Oxford (1932)
Webb, T. W.: The Civil War in Herefordshire (1879)
Wood, A. C.: Nottinghamshire in the Civil War (1937)

Biographies
Adair, J.: Roundhead General (Sir William Waller (1969)
Ashley, M.: Cromwell (1969)
Ashley, M.: Cromwell's Generals (1964)
Berry, J. and Lee, S. G.: A Cromwellian Major-General: The Career of Colonel James Berry (1935)
Buchan, J.: Cromwell (1934)

Jones, J. R.: Booth's Rising of 1659
Buchan, J.: The Marquis of Montrose (1928)
Dawson, W. H.: Cromwell's Understudy. The Life and Times of General Lambert (1938)
Edgar, F. T. R.: Sir Ralph Hopton. The King's Man in the West (1968)
Ferguson, B.: Rupert of the Rhine (1952)
Firth, C. H.: The Life of William Cavendish, Duke of Newcastle (1886)
Firth, C. H.: Oliver Cromwell (1929)
Firth, C. H.: The Memoirs of Edmund Ludlow (1894)
Gibb, M. A.: The Lord General (Sir Thomas Fairfax) (1938)
Granville, R.: The King's General in the West. The Life of Sir Richard Granville (1908)
Hutchinson, L.: Memoirs of the Life of Colonel Hutchinson (1965)
Kaufman, H. A.: Conscientious Cavalier. Colonel Bullen Reymes (1962)
Markham, C. R.: A Life of the Great Lord Fairfax (1870)
Maurice, F.: The Adventures of Edward Wogan (1945)
Ramsey, R. W.: Henry Ireton (1949)
Scott, E.: Rupert, Prince Palatinate (1899)
Smith, G. R.: Without Touch of Dishonour (Sir Henry Slingsby) (1968)
Terry, C. S.: The Life and Campaigns of Alexander Leslie, First Earl of Leven (1899)
Tibbutt, H. G.: Colonel John Okey 1606–1662 (1955)
Toynbee, M.: King Charles I (1968)
Tucker, N.: Royalist Major General, Sir John Owen (1963)
Verney, P.: The Standard Bearer (Sir Edward Verney) (1964)
Warburton, E.: Memoirs of Prince Rupert and the Cavaliers (1849)
Wedgewood, C. V.: Montrose (1952)
Wedgewood, C. V.: Oliver Cromwell (1947)
Wilkinson, C.: Prince Rupert, the Cavalier (1934)
Williamson, H. R.: Charles and Cromwell (1946)
Young, P.: Oliver Cromwell and his Times (1962)
Young, P.: Cromwell (1968)
Young, P. and Tucker, N.: The Civil War. Richard Atkyns and John Gwyn (1967)

Miscellaneous Specialist Works
Hall, A. R.: Ballistics in the Seventeenth Century (1952)
Powell, J. R.: The Navy in the English Civil War (1962)
Solt, L. F.: Saints in Arms (Chaplains in the Parliamentary Army) (1959)
Winstock, L. S.: Songs and Marches of the Roundheads and Cavaliers (1971)
Underdown, D.: Royalist Conspiracy in England 1649–1660 (1960)
Powell, J. H. and Timings, E. K.: Documents relating to the Civil War (1963)

Soc
DA
415
T797

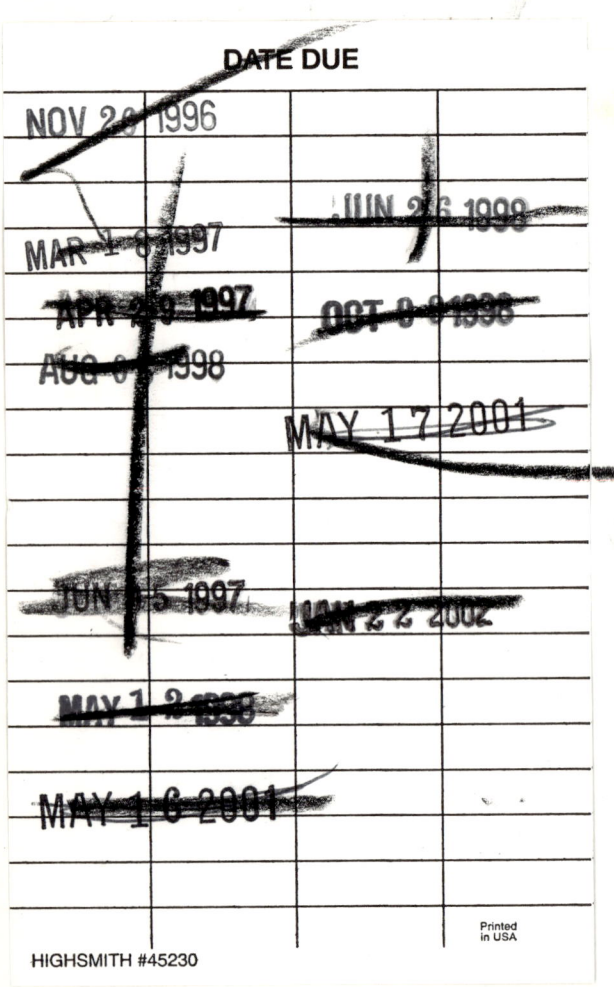